Twayne's United States Authors Series

EDITOR OF THIS VOLUME

Warren French

Indiana University

Howard Nemerov

TUSAS 356

HOWARD NEMEROV

By ROSS LABRIE

University of British Columbia

TWAYNE PUBLISHERS

A DIVISION OF G. K. HALL & CO., BOSTON

811.54
M7433zl

Published in 1980 by Twayne Publishers,
A Division of G. K. Hall & Co.
All Rights Reserved

Printed on permanent/durable acid-free paper and bound
in the United States of America

First Printing

Frontispiece photo of Howard Nemerov courtesy of
Washington University Photographic Services,
St. Louis, Missouri

Library of Congress Cataloging in Publication Data

Labrie, Ross.
Howard Nemerov.

(Twayne's United States authors series; TUSAS 356)
Bibliography: p. 151-154
Includes index.
1.   Nemerov, Howard—
Criticism and interpretation.
PS3527.E5Z74   811'.5'4   79-17632
ISBN 0-8057-7298-7

for Mark and Steven

Contents

About the Author

Ross Labrie teaches American literature in the Department of English at the University of British Columbia in Vancouver. He received his Ph.D. from the University of Toronto in 1966. He taught for one year at the University of Saskatchewan before joining the faculty of the University of British Columbia.

He has published a number of articles on Henry James, Thomas Merton, and on the literature of the 1920s in journals such as *American Literature*, the *Arizona Quarterly*, the *North Dakota Quarterly*, *Renascence*, *Greyfriar*, the *Lakehead University Review*, the *Canadian Review of American Studies*, and *Resources for American Literary Study*.

In recent years Prof. Labrie has become increasingly interested in twentieth century American poetry, particularly in poetry written since 1945. His book, *The Art of Thomas Merton*, which was published by Texas Christian University Press in 1979, in addition to focusing on Merton's narrative writing, essays, and journals, presented a detailed examination of Merton's poetic theory and practice. The book followed a year's research in Louisville, Kentucky where most of Merton's manuscripts are located.

The present volume on Howard Nemerov was made possible by a research grant from the Canada Council in 1977. The grant enabled Prof. Labrie to travel to St. Louis in order to talk to Nemerov about his writing and in order to study those manuscripts of Nemerov's which are housed at Washington University. An interview with Nemerov, which was recorded while Prof. Labrie was in St. Louis, was published in the *Southern Review* in the summer of 1979.

Preface

Howard Nemerov's induction into the prestigious American Academy of Arts and Letters in 1977 marked the culmination of a writing career that has included some of the richest poetry and most accomplished fiction of the postwar period. He emerged in the 1940s between the reign of Pound and Eliot and the later schools of the Beats and the Black Mountain poets. His emergence in the interval between two prominent periods of poetry helped, along with his traditionalism, to conceal his worth during the 1950s and 1960s. In the last ten years, however, his contribution to modern letters has been recognized in full-length studies of his poetry. The present book is intended to provide a detailed introduction to the full range of his writings—poetry, fiction, and criticism.

Nemerov's distinctiveness as a contemporary writer lies in the eloquent attention he has given to the moment of perception. In this connection both his poetry and fiction are informed by a sophisticated understanding of contemporary epistemology. Metaphysical emanations are vividly tied to the experience of consciousness as it gazes outward at the mysteries of the external world before looking inward at the even greater mystery of itself. In exploring the contemporary mood of disaffected skepticism and metaphysical loneliness, Nemerov has quietly illuminated important aspects of the intellectual and spiritual temper of America in the last thirty years.

I am grateful to Howard Nemerov for the time he has taken to discuss his work with me both in person and through correspondence. I am also indebted to Holly Hall of the Special Collections section of the Olin Library at Washington University in St. Louis for her help in researching Nemerov's manuscripts and letters. In addition, I acknowledge the permission of Washington University to quote from manuscripts in the Special Collections section of the Olin Library. Finally, I wish to thank the Canada Council for the grant that enabled me to travel to St. Louis to talk with Nemerov and to complete my research.

Ross Labrie

University of British Columbia

Chronology

1920   Howard Nemerov born March 1, New York City. His father, David Nemerov, the president and chairman of the board of Russek's, an exclusive New York clothing store, had a reputation as a connoisseur of art in addition to being an amateur painter and philanthropist. Nemerov's mother, Gertrude, was a member of the Russek family. There were three children: Howard, Diane (now dead)—who, as Diane Arbus became a photographer of note—and Renée.

1937   Graduated from the exclusive Fieldston School in New York and entered Harvard.

1941   Graduated from Harvard with a B.A., having won the Bowdoin Essay Prize in 1940. His senior essay on Thomas Mann received praise from Mann himself.

1941   Enlists in the Royal Canadian Air Force and serves as a fighter pilot in the Royal Air Force Coastal Command; from 1944 to 1945 serves with the Eighth U.S. Army Air Force.

1944   Marries Margaret Russell, an English woman, January 26. They are to have three sons: David, Alexander, and Jeremy.

1946   Appointed Instructor of English at Hamilton College, Clinton, N.Y.

1946 -
1951   Associate editor of *Furioso* under Reed Whittemore.

1947   *The Image and the Law*, first book of poems.

1948   Joins Faculty of Literature and Languages at Bennington College, where he teaches regularly until 1958, remaining formally attached to the college until 1966. His colleagues include Kenneth Burke, Reed Whittemore, Stanley Edgar Hyman, and Bernard Malamud.

1949   *The Melodramatists*, first novel.

1950   *Guide to the Ruins* (poems).

1954   *Federigo, or the Power of Love* (novel).

1955   *The Salt Garden* (poems).

1957   *The Homecoming Game,* a novel, later made into the film *Tall Story* (1960), which turns out to be a lucrative source of income for Nemerov.

1958   *Mirrors and Windows* (poems); receives the Blumenthal Prize from *Poetry* magazine; visiting lecturer in English at the University of Minnesota for 1958 - 1959.

1959   *A Commodity of Dreams* (short stories).

1960   *New & Selected Poems,* which contains "Runes," a poetic sequence which Nemerov has identified as his favorite work.

1962   *The Next Room of the Dream* (poems); contains two verse plays, "Endor" and "Cain"; writer-in-residence at Hollins College in Virginia, 1962 - 1963.

1963   *Poetry & Fiction* (essays); appointed consultant in poetry to the Library of Congress for one year.

1965   *Journal of the Fictive Life* (autobiography).

1966   Appointed Professor of English at Brandeis University in Massachusetts.

1967   *The Blue Swallows* (poems), which earns Nemerov the Theodore Roethke Memorial Prize.

1969   Hurst Professor of Literature at Washington University in St. Louis; subsequently joins the Department of English at Washington University as Professor of English.

1971   *Stories, Fables & Other Diversions.*

1972   *Reflections on Poetry & Poetics* (essays).

1973   *Gnomes & Other Occasions* (poems).

1975   *The Western Approaches* (poems).

1977   *Collected Poems;* honored by induction into the American Academy of Arts and Letters.

CHAPTER 1

Nemerov's Approach to Art

I Biographical Background

O N the dustjacket of his novel *The Melodramatists* Nemerov
has described his background as "dignified, commonplace, and
thoroughly middle-class." In spite of the archness in tone the
description is apt. Emerging from an affluent, conservative family
background, he is essentially the Jewish Puritan of the middle class
he has characterized himself as being in the autobiographical
Journal of the Fictive Life. Among other things the characterization
explains his being one of the most industrious writers of his time, a
man who has been frequently described as happy only when he is
writing: "The process of writing almost always makes me happy;
the results, only sometimes. I have found poetic imagination to be
chiefly a matter of waiting, and sometimes what one waits for turns
out to be trivial enough; but there's no help for that. If in a fit of
pride I decide to write only what is important, or useful, or
heroically large, the Muse simply packs up and goes South for a
long winter."[1]

Nemerov has freely admitted his conservatism, having confided
on one occasion that a revolutionary situation in the arts didn't suit
him.[2] In spite of his insistent need to write, to publish, and to be
successful, he has found himself at the mercy of a pervasive
melancholy throughout his life, a voice within that scowls at the
record of achievement, noting dryly that success in art is no great
matter since art itself—literary art, at any rate—has a questionable
future and that the "entire industry, captains and crooks together, is
failing."[3]

Except for his flying in World War II, Nemerov has led a rather
uneventful life, most of it within the confines of academia. He enjoys teaching, and this appears to provide him with as much in-

tellectualizing and socializing as he needs. Without avoiding
literary conversation, he has said that he does not require it and is
happiest working on his own at home. A number of his poems show
him stirring about within his house listening to sounds or staring out
of the window. Like a number of American poets who came along
in the 1940s, he has not identified with any particular literary movement. He dislikes the rigidity of such groups, and has not been particularly sympathetic to the Beats or the Black Mountain school for
example. He has preferred the path of the solitary and the eclectic,
identifying rather shyly with people like Robert Frost, whose poetry
has had a noticeable influence on his work.

Recognizing the dangers for the creative writer in being a
teacher, Nemerov has contended that without academics there
would be few readers of poetry. The danger that he sees in teaching
is that the teacher's penchant for explaining might carry over into
his writing of poetry and fiction. The way around this, he has main-
tained, is for the poet or novelist to concentrate not on his ideas or
his knowledge but on himself—drawing on the sometimes uncom-
fortable, personal imagery that arises from experience.

Nemerov's years teaching at Bennington College in Vermont
were especially important in reconciling his roles as teacher, poet,
novelist and critic. In this small college he found himself among
some of the most fertile minds of his time, including Kenneth
Burke, Bernard Malamud, Reed Whittemore, and Stanley Edgar
Hyman, scholars who had a relaxed, experimental and yet richly
theoretical approach to art. He liked his colleagues' approach to
teaching and criticism, describing the approach to art taken at Bennington during the 1950s as inductive and unsystematic. It was an
approach that addressed itself to the illumination of works and ideas
without trying to channel such discussion so that it fitted neatly into
literary periods and genres. Nemerov's own criticism reflects the
Bennington approach, reflecting both scrupulousness and
generosity.

Asked about influences on his work, Nemerov has replied that he
has had them all. He has, though, singled out favorites—
Shakespeare, Socrates, Montaigne, Freud—regarding Freud in particular as one of the great poets. He has visualized his relationship
to other writers and indeed to other fields of knowledge such as science as that of the packrat foraging for food. Culture, like the world
itself, is there for the writer to use: "It occurs to me," he once ob-

served, "that I treat the world as if it were one giant waiting room. I'm waiting for it to bring in its next entertainment."⁴

Judaism has had a considerable influence on Nemerov's approach to art and it figures prominently in a number of his poems and stories. Although he has no particular interest in formal religion, he does uphold his Jewishness. While analyzing himself in *Journal of the Fictive Life,* for instance, he wrote: "Better off with the Jew Freud, tell your dreams in his style . . . he tells you life is tough and doesn't promise anything; while Jung, the Christian mystagogue, will give you a lot of Hollywood death imagery that looks consoling but will turn out to be the same old savagery in the end.⁵ He has acknowledged that the stories of the Old Testament had a profound effect on him in his youth and had much to do with his feeling for life as a magical, mysterious process. While he is aware of the skeptical tenor of his time, he has argued that skepticism sterilizes the artist whereas the attitude of belief, with whatever ingenuousness is part of it, is more likely to be fertile.

Hence, he often adopts an informal religious attitude toward art and the creative process. The artist, like Adam in paradise, is the *"namer of the world."*⁶ Nemerov tends frequently to invest the creative process with the language of the visionary. The artist waits in humility for the world to speak to him. Then the imagination becomes active, marshalling sound, picture, and rhythm in order to express what he has received. The artist must take care not to disturb the sanctity of the creative moment. Nemerov has noted that, in composing poetry, he never liked to leave his desk before he had finished a complete draft: "I never knew what I wanted to write before it began to appear; the line, the cadence, the formal problem, always or almost always preceded anything that might be called 'the idea.' "⁷ The readiness was all. The artist remained attentive to nature and the sounds which subtly interfused both the world and the impending poem would register themselves in a process that Nemerov has called "miraculous." ⁸

II   *The Role of the Artist*

Nemerov has described artists as helping the rest of mankind to "see in a thinking way."⁹ The emphasis is on perception, the delicate, suspended apprehension of the world by the mind. The artist would help the reader to see the world freshly and with new

attentiveness, seeing for the first time perhaps things which the eye
had often scanned without recognizing. The artist not only mirrors
the world, but shapes it as well by changing the vision of those who
move through it. Thus, Nemerov sees *Hamlet* as having altered the
character and destinies of human beings for the last 400 years.

The artist introduces the reader to the strangeness of the world.
The purpose of this is to prepare humanity for fresh, future encoun-
ters with that raw, active world that lies forever beyond our simplified patterns of thought. In this sense art is a border activity, an
advance party which operates on the perimeter between our present
knowledge and methods of perception and "whatever mysterious
and probably dangerous unknowns" await us on the "far side of
poetry, of literature, of all that we call art."[10] The literary artist also
operates in a border area in that he uses language, the membranous
world between thought and thing. Language helps the artist to
come tangibly close to experience. In this connection, Nemerov has
admired works like Joyce's *Finnegans Wake* for showing "how
bodily a thing language really is."[11]

The artist registers the odd and habitual gravitation of the mind
toward the belief that human beings have a place in the scheme of
things, even when science blandly insists upon the ultimate ar-
bitrariness and meaninglessness of their lives. Similarly, while art
depicts the pain and defeat, it also caresses the mind by registering
pain in the "richest and loveliest and most pleasure-bearing language" so that suffering and loss are presented under the aspects of
"power, heroism, nobility, courage and courtesy and love—and, of
course, illusion."[12] The artist's method parallels the poignancy of
his vision: "We write, at last, because life is hopeless and
beautiful."[13]

III *Perception and Language*

One of the recurring figures in Nemerov's poetry is the medieval
scholastic philosopher William of Ockham, whom he characterizes
as the father of modern skepticism. Ockham pointed out that there
is an unbridgeable chasm between the mind and external reality,
the inner and the outer world. Though unsystematic in his approach, Nemerov has kept abreast of epistemological philosophy
since Ockham's time and his own work might be regarded as a
further chapter in the history of that rather esoteric field of study.

He sees the Romantics as having opened the question up in a

dramatic way as a challenge to the post-Renaissance bias toward empiricism in Western culture. Romantics like Wordsworth and Coleridge seized upon perception as a central interest precisely because it had become "problematic and doubtful." [14] Nemerov has felt that epistemological questions have been treated in a cursory way by contemporary American poets and novelists, Wallace Stevens being an honorable exception. This disregard has often led to a hastily adopted empiricism on the part of artists who feel unable to fathom the philosophical issues involved or to defend the value of their own thought. The distrust of thought itself has led, Nemerov believes, to the emergence of movements like Imagism in poetry which leave little room for the display of the mind.

For Nemerov the first step in valuing thought is to become aware of its pervasiveness. One comes to recognize that thought, imagination, the mind are all inextricably part of what is called reality, the means whereby one comes to know reality and hence inseparable from it. If the mind is fated to see itself involved in whatever external phenomenon it contemplates, it may also celebrate itself in recognizing its own creativity.

Nemerov finally asserts the existence and value of spiritual knowledge, but with characteristic reserve indicates that such an idealization of the world is in a sense a "silly" belief, even if it is "upon that silliness that human life, as distinct from the life of beasts, chiefly depends." [15] The mind, however, has no alternative. It can either submit to the chaos of particulars which comprises the outer world or it can attempt to order things into some sort of meaning, risking thereby the distortion of reality and inevitably projecting itself helplessly into that which it would study and order. For Nemerov this is not a problem peculiar to the arts and the humanities, but is inherent in all knowledge, including science. The paradoxical advantage of the artist over the scientist in this age lies in his readiness to perceive the universal subjectivity of all knowledge. In his essay "Poetry, Prophecy, Prediction" Nemerov has observed that scientific language is the language in which we "tell each other myths about the motions and the purposes of mind disguised as world, as time, as truth," adding dryly that "myth believed is never called a myth." [16]

The terms in which Nemerov pictures his absorbing epistemological puzzle are those of the eye and the mind, the eye being closest to the authentic shapes and sound of the external world, the mind regally aloof in abstracting subtle thoughts from the eye's harvest of particulars. Both are indispensable in successful perception, because, in spite of its vanity, the mind is required to allow men to not only see but to see through the things which appear before them. Their seeing through may eventually involve some visionary perceptions, but the contact by the mind with things invisible begins long before that. The invisible, Nemerov writes, "does not begin with God, the gods, and such high matters; it begins much closer to home, wherever pattern is discriminated and relationship inferred."[17] Ideally, the eye rests upon the object before it with "attentiveness and obedience," to use a phrase which Nemerov borrowed from Thomas Mann, but the mind wants to push forward, assimilating, relating, transforming, and symbolizing, pursuing the secret which it knows to be there.

The drama of perception is the primary subject of Nemerov's poetry and it inevitably involves the attempt to reconcile mind and eye with each other and both with external reality—the inner and outer worlds. For Nemerov art is the experience of thought in nature. With its allegiance both to things and to the mind art entices thought back into relation with the senses and with the physical world. Thus, art is a mediator between subject and object, an attempt in the most sublime sense to "pray one's humanity back into the universe; and conversely an attempt to read, to derive anew, one's humanity from nature."[18] Art interfuses thought and things in a momentary apprehension—a "great reckoning in a little room."[19]

An esoteric benefit for the mind that becomes aware of itself traveling out to objects in order to illuminate them is that it can study not only the objects with which it combines, but itself as well—incarnated in the physical world. This sort of perception by the mind of itself underlies many of Nemerov's finest poems, poems which he calls *reflexive*. What might have been seen, therefore, as a liability from an epistemological point of view—the indissoluble interpenetration of mind and reality—becomes an advantage to the artist seeking to explore the configurations of consciousness.

If the attitude which holds the inner and outer worlds in balance is attentiveness, the mind's homage to the richness of the external world, the instrument which will help the writer register this balance is language. The danger with language is that, being a kind of emissary of the mind and of civilization, it may already have so digested the outer world that dictionaries themselves may be thought to contain nothing but solipsistic information. Man's reading of the world around him, then, may already be radically literary, tipping the epistemological balance of things in the direction of mind and illusion. In an essay, significantly entitled "This Babel and Beyond," Nemerov argues that man inherits his language, a language which is a sort of museum of man's history and thought, without having the chance of not accepting the inheritance. Language, then, by reflecting the selective consciousness and histories of the generations of those who composed it, imposes "fictitious distinctions upon the continuouness of things, especially by dividing qualities into pairs of opposites."[20]

Nemerov has found himself agreeing with Freud that words are a halfway house to lost things. In this sense the poem or novel is independent of the mind of its creator, who may well find it as mysterious as anyone else. He believes that the poet writes a poem not to say what he thinks, nor even to find out what he thinks, but instead "to find out what *it* thinks."[21] Since language exists independently of the writer's mind, as well as within it, it has something of the strangeness of the outer world and can be shaped to reflect the sense of strangeness elicited by that world. For Nemerov language becomes a substantial world in itself, a world in which "we trade with the words, we push them back and forth, mysterious entities not things but more powerful than things to make us angry or sad, elated, anxious, confused, to make us mighty in battle, weak in peace, pushovers to our enemies and a holy terror to people we have never met."[22] In a major essay, "Attentiveness and Obedience," he has written eloquently about the world generated by language: "I do not now, if I ever did, consent to the common modern view of language as a system of conventional signs for the passive reception of experience, but tend ever more to see language as making an unknowably large part of a material world whose independent existence might be likened to that of the human unconscious, a sleep of causes, a chaos of the possible—impossible, responsive only to the wakening touch of desire and fear—that is, to spirit; that is, to the word."[23]

Nemerov concedes both the unknowableness of being and his fascination with perception. The tension between these two polarized views is resolved in his writing by his consuming interest in illusion. He has written in another major essay, "The Swaying Form," that language can be seen as a "marvelous mirror of the human condition, a mirror so miraculous that it can see what is invisible, that is, the relations between things."[24] It is this capacity to perceive relations that is the glory of the imagination and its mysterious instrument, language. In spite of the awesome otherness of nature, the artist's imagination is able to vibrate sympathetically with a tree, a river, a swallow in such a way that he learns something of what it means to live in the world as tree, river, swallow, and man. In rare, ecstatic moments Nemerov goes so far as to attribute a kind of parallel consciousness to nature, knowing nonetheless that he is courting illusion.

With the whole of civilization reflected in it, language is the visible area where relations are perceived and generated, thereby bringing about the incarnation through the word, as Nemerov sees it, the uniting of the material and immaterial worlds. The relations and cross-relations between things, often developed by means of penetrating analogies, are for Nemerov the very essence of the artist's work and are clearly both the method and subject of most of his writing. In its most refined state, Nemerov's poetry involves meditation upon the art of relating by analogy, poems about writing poems. The unifying of perception brought about by brilliant analogies can involve not only the outer and inner worlds and not only the mind and the eye, but through the cultural content of language can bind together the laws of nature and those of human history.

IV   Art and Meaning

Nemerov wrote on one occasion that the deepest and most difficult question to be asked of poetry was: "Is it a sacrament or a con game? Echo answers."[25] His characteristic balancing of skepticism and belief has led him to tread carefully, if hopefully, in exploring the meaning of art. He has been guided here as always by a deep-seated distrust of the vanity of the mind, which all too readily admires its own creations and which is all too eager to invest them with meaning. The mind's thirst for meaning is unquenchable, and although Nemerov has celebrated the inventiveness of the mind, he is generally uncomfortably aware of its tendency to monopolize experience by absorbing and transforming particulars until they lose their concreteness and become immaterial subtleties caught up in the mind's relentless reordering of the external world: "For example, in children's playbooks there are numbered dots to be followed in sequence by the pencil; the line so produced finally becomes recognizable as a shape. So the lines produced among stars (which can scarcely all be in the same plane) become the geometrical abstractions of a Bear, a Wagon, Orion the Hunter; and by softening or humanizing the outlines, recognizable images are produced, but in the process the stars themselves have to be omitted. So does meaning at first simplify and afterward supersede the world."[26]

On the other hand Nemerov has balked at the empirical practice of many contemporary critics in ignoring the meaning of a literary work in favor of an exhaustive and often sterile examination of technique, particularly among the too earnest descendants of the New Critics. For Nemerov meaning and value have an obvious place in art. Unlike the Imagists, he has no strong objection to the moralizing of late nineteenth-century poetry; what he objects to is the fact that the morality propounded in this poetry was simplistic and overly abstract. Nevertheless, he believes that the artist becomes significant not when he communicates values, but when his work becomes a value in itself. At this point readers cease to judge the artist's work in the light of their own experience and begin to judge their experience in the light of the artist's work.

Fundamentally, Nemerov has a tolerant view of literary tradition, seeing and valuing a variety of different styles. His descriptions of art tend to have plenty of latitude. Ultimately, the best artistic work, he believes, will mirror the world and experience rather than the world's or the artist's opinions. The art object registers the "silence behind the language, the silence within the language."[27] Thus, while art may point in the direction of meaning, it does not, at least in its finest form, announce these meanings.

Nevertheless, much of Nemerov's own poetry involves a good deal of philosophizing. His strategy for this sort of writing is to be what he calls *pre-Socratic,* thinking in fragments rather than as part of an enclosed, highly developed system of thought. In this way the thinking in the poems will inevitably contradict itself, a healthy sign of the mind's independence from the regime of its own created, ordering systems. He has, in fact, felt himself tempted to view art, especially poetry, as a place where contradictions do not destroy one another. Moreover, he has insisted that the philosophical views found in his poems are not to be taken as maxims, even when they sound that way, but are rather to be regarded as views which have crystallized at the particular moment in that particular poem with its own set of internal and external circumstances. Speaking of the composition of his poem "The Winter Lightning" he observed: "When I speak of poetry as a cold art, you have to remember that that comes out of the occasion of walking out in a snowstorm and seeing lightning looking very cold, colder than snow. So it's not the same lesson that would be taught by walking out in a thunderstorm in June."[28]

Nemerov has drawn attention to the ironic parallel between the proliferation of sophisticated knowledge in contemporary society and the collapse in the idea of meaning. Similarly, he has argued, the thousands of those who are now studying the creative process have not observably been turning into artists. Amidst the burgeoning of knowledge, the artist is cautioned to be rigorously selective. In addition, his creations should be regarded as explorations of the possible and even the impossible rather than that which has been certified by science. The materials in a story or poem may appear meaningless at first until the reader adjusts his eyes to the artist's way of seeing. This may well involve seeing not the titled subject itself, but an earlier, incomplete stage of the subject caught in a moment of its slow state of development. Furthermore, sifting among various rival truths, the artist will settle for none, finally, but will permit a chosen few to reveal their inner vitality. In this way, Nemerov argues, the poem or story is more like the movement of the mind than like the thoughts which the mind contains.

As part of the latitude of his approach Nemerov has compared the workings of art to those of both science and religion. Art is seen as in its own way approaching the precision of science, even in the realm of the impossible and invented. He has visualized Shakespeare, for example, as asking the question of Othello: what will be the result if this nobler nature can be led to believe Desdemona unfaithful? Shakespeare thus sets up a sort of experiment, keeping an eye on irrelevancies that must be excluded if the experiment is to proceed under controlled conditions. Both art and religion operate on the perimeter of the visible and invisible worlds and both are enthralled by the strangeness of the world. Ironically, though, religion submits to dogma, causing its pristine vision to shrink and ossify, whereas the artist, by not stopping at any one revelation, keeps his vision liquid and open to change. For Nemerov formal religion is particularly vulnerable in pretending to knowledge about the real world rather than submitting to the inspired moment in wonder and acknowledged ignorance.

V   *Artistic Form*

Nemerov conceives of art as a dream. The art object is a dream
first of all in its shape, its anti-logical, anti-linear outline. He frequently speaks of the art object as combining the circle and the line,
the circle of form that eventually illuminates the line of meaning. In
this respect he has compared the action of the art object to the
tracking of a phonograph needle across a record. Similarly, in the
essay "Poetry, Prophecy, Prediction" he has noted that in poetical
thought the "shortest way between two points is through a
labyrinth."[29] Indirectness and suggestiveness are the circular idiom
of the artist's dreamscape, thus paralleling the shape of experience:
"We do not ordinarily believe we make progress by going 'round in
circles; and yet in a round world we may have no other course. Consider how it is precisely, though mysteriously, the circling of the
heavens that creates time, whose even progress along a straight line
is among the blandest of our metaphysical assumptions."[30]

The art object is a dream in that it temporarily and mysteriously
mingles the wish fulfillment of the author and the relatively hard
elements of the external world. On rare occasions even raw experience shows itself, Nemerov believes, as having the "interpretable
depth" of a dream, but when this happens life simply takes on the
"transpicuousness" of art, even while keeping its own "weight and
solid specificity."[31] In general, however, the artist's imagination is
required to form the circle of concrete particulars with its inherent
line of meaning. The motif of the poem as dream is paralleled in
Nemerov's conception of art to that of the child's vision. If the artist
is childlike, he is also sophisticated in being aware of the ingenuous
nature of all knowledge. The artist recovers for all men, however, a
paradisal vision of the world, using language as it had been used in
the "few hours between Adam's naming the creation and his fall."[32]

Nemerov connects the image of the art object as dream with
the prophetic role of the artist: "This kind of prophecy does not
predict, it is never precise, it does not specify particulars or give
dates; it dreams on things to come. And dreams, as everyone knows
so well these days, do not work by fact and reason but by wish and
fear, by wish inseparable from fear. . . . The poet is in the ancient
word for him a *maker*, and he doesn't foretell the future, he makes
it, he brings it to pass, he sings it up. It becomes his dream."[33] The
artist thus appeals to man as dreamer, believer, and storyteller. The

name given to the most abiding of man's stories is myth. Myths are
prime, archetypal patterns of human experience, but in a sense they
are also simply the sort of dream stories which artists tell, stories
which are generated, like the stories in the Old Testament, in the
"violence of individuals" and in "generation and choice" rather
than in the historian's abstract patterns of description.[34] Nemerov
sees history as a continuum which the historian chooses to arti-
ficially divide into beginnings and endings and into collective and
abstract events.

The artist's mythic tale on the other hand holds to the continuum
of experience, presenting life as a seamless and ritualistically
repetitive dream in which, rather than focusing on beginnings and
endings, the artist concentrates on surfaces and depths in his attempt to illuminate the present. Myth is at once emblematic and
mysterious, tracing the subtle laws which lead inexorably to particular destinies and yet remaining ultimately enigmatic. Although initially influenced by the New Critics, Nemerov later came to perceive poems and stories as talismans that embodied the "magical, il-
lusionist, or religious character of art, which has customarily rested
on the assumption that God in creating the world did something
coherent although mysterious, and that therefore history, at the last
great day, would be seen as 'like'a drama."[35]

On a textual level the artist's shaping of sound and picture captures the hypnotic aspects of the dreamscape so that the intellect is
forced once again to abandon or at least suspend its determined,
linear rationalism. Sound and rhythm bring about the sort of primary, subconscious pleasure which, even if it elicits the intellect's
contempt, may still lead the reader to the most profoundly felt
truths: "The painter Delacroix expressed it by saying that Nature is
a dictionary. Everything is there, but not in the order one needs.
The universe itself, so far as we relate ourselves to it by the mind,
may be not so much a meaning as a rhythm, a continuous articulation of question and answer . . . a musical dialectic precipitating
out moments of meaning which become distinct only as one wave
does in a sea of waves. 'You think you live under universal princi-
ples,' said Montaigne, 'but in fact they are municipal bylaws.' "[36]

The writer hopes that by bringing language as close as possible to
the condition of music he can conceal meaning within the body language of the poem until it is felt so strongly that trying to understand it would seem redundant. The depths from which sound and
rhythm emerge begin far back within the poet's psychic history,

and, inasmuch as he uses language, far back in the origins and history of humanity. In "The Measure of Poetry" Nemerov traces the rhythms which eventually appear in a poem to a place "far out in the sea of tradition and the mind, even in the physiological deeps, where some empty, echoing, abstract interval begins to beat."[37] The rhythmic energy released within the artist's psyche is not relayed directly to the poem but is drawn into the concrete particulars of the artist's subject. Through language it emerges in a final, transformed state, like the breaking of a wave on shore, a wave that had its origin in the dark depths of the ocean.

Nemerov views the art object as organic in the sense that diverse materials within it are fused by the streaming of sound, rhythm, and picture into a satisfying whole in a more intimate manner than could be achieved by conventional grammatical structuring. Nevertheless, he views his poetry as quite distinct from the organic poetry heralded by William Carlos Williams, Robert Creeley and a number of recent poets. He sees the poem in a fairly traditional way as a formal structure, even an impersonal one in T.S. Eliot's sense. Furthermore, he regards the poem as reflecting the matured perceptions of the poet. He uses devices like metaphor, meter, and paradox in a traditional manner. Although he does not identify with Eliot's dourness and allusiveness, he has been greatly influenced by Eliot's insistence upon intellectual rigor in the artist.

In this connection he has described the Beat poets as sloppy, and after reading some open form poetry in the 1960s in an anthology entitled *Naked Poetry*, he announced: "I think I'll go read some clothed couplets, especially if they have a sweet disorder in the dress."[38] Similarly, he has objected to Dylan Thomas's poetry because of its looseness in form: "the energy has nothing to hold it back, it is under no pressure from the theoretical pattern of the line (which it has almost but not quite destroyed), so that the tension and sinuosity are lost, and the energetic impulsion which begins the line either cracks up or proceeds merely as shouting; nor does any intensification of assonance and so forth overcome this difficulty."[39]

Not hiding his conservatism, Nemerov has expressed pleasure at the question-and-answer format of some of Shakespeare's sonnets because this imposes limits upon the poetic journey. In addition, with respect to diction, he has dissociated himself from those who try to ignore dictionary meanings and also from those who stress the use of American rather than English speech. His comment on this affectation is memorably witty: "As for An American Language

Distinct from English, if people want to write poems in that language, fine. But if they want to argue with you about it and the room hasn't got a door, you listen to what they have to say as patiently as possible and then ask them to say it over in American. Mostly these slogans amount to edicts decreeing that from now on you should walk on one foot only."[40]

In Nemerov's view art characteristically involves a tension between polarities, ultimately those of energy and order. He objected to the San Francisco group of poets of the 1950s and 1960s—Ferlinghetti, for example—on the grounds that their work is not dialectical enough. Similarly, he has found some of James Dickey's poems wanting in that their "dreaming lucidities" are sometimes too "relaxed."[41] The advantage of a dialectical approach is not only its heightening of form, but its enhancement of theme as well. Through this method, Nemerov believes, philosophically opposed entities—like love and war—may be placed next to each other so that they become complexly interfused as they do in experience, if not in the mind. Without abandoning his sense of the literary work as a dialectical structure, he later came to stress simplicity in form as a primary value and the "detachment of a single thought from its ambiguous surroundings as a worthier object than the deliberate cultivation of ambiguity."[42]

With respect to literary form Nemerov has identified with few writers as strongly as with John Crowe Ransom, writing favorably of Ransom's precision, urbanity, and his avoidance of sentimentality, all of which he has striven for in his own work. He has summed up the effect of Ransom's poems as essentially one of elegance, including in this both Ransom's meticulous technical accomplishment and his refined observations. The danger of the writer's devotion to elegance, that he might surpass the intellectual reach of his readers, is something which on the whole Nemerov appears willing to risk:

If poetry reaches the point which chess has reached, where the decisive, profound, and elegant combinations lie within the scope only of masters, and are appreciable only to competent and trained players, that will seem to many people a sorry state of affairs, and to some people a consequence simply of the sinfulness of poets; but it will not in the least mean that poetry is, as they say, *dead;* rather the reverse. It is when poetry becomes altogether too easy, too accessible, runs down to a few derivative formulae and caters to low tastes and lazy minds—it is then that the life of the art is in danger.[43]

Nemerov has taken pains to stress the need in a work of art for both concrete particulars and for the symbolic reverberations of these particulars. The poem or novel thus mediates between the visible world of objects and the invisible world of relations and meanings so that the pleasure obtained from reading is in seeing "minds flower *in* their facts."[44] Ransom again is a model of balance in this respect, focusing on local incidents and rendering characters and their situations specifically rather than giving himself over to reflection. Nemerov has tried to root his own poems in concrete particulars, most notably in poems like "The Mud Turtle" and "The Pond." On the other hand one of his objections to Imagism is that it allows poems to get bogged down in the elaboration of concrete particulars. While he admires the Imagists' ability to precisely describe the hard, sharp surfaces of things, he feels that there has been an unfortunate suppression of subjective elements, particularly with respect to the articulation of perceived relationships. Similarly, he has tended to regard the fragmentary collage technique espoused by many contemporary poets as a facile escape from the need to carefully integrate imagery with the musical, syntactical, and intellectual organization of the poem.

Nemerov's conception of metaphor is a traditional Romantic one: "Poetry is an art of combination, or discovering the secret valencies which the most widely differing things have for one another."[45] He makes it clear that the creation of a metaphor, the interfusion of thought and thing, is a penetration of reality. Since metaphors are constructed of concrete particulars drawn from the external world, the reader has a good deal of freedom in responding to the proposed metaphorical analogy, using his own experience with these particulars as a criterion. The more specific the particulars the better, whether drawn from external nature or history. The name of a thing in either case carries with it an "obstinate singularity and irreducibility of tradition and history, which have happened once and do not repeat themselves and so have an immense overplus of being in addition to whatever they possess and yield of meaning."[46] Thus, for Nemerov the name of a thing both refreshes and eludes the mind with its solidity and its existential independence:

we cannot understand a name until we understand something else; and that something else is most often a unique and particular something else, something that happened, or is said to have happened, only once, and which therefore does not enter language as a generality. . . . Hence, whether names are or are not in the first instance arbitrary, they bring something arbitrary into discourse, something obstinately unyielding: bringing in the individual, they bring in history, or tradition, and the stern idea of a world in which things happen once and for all.[47]

While allowing his metaphor to resonate with whatever meanings it can generate, the prudent artist, Nemerov believes, will halt the process at the point where excitement and delight appear to be turning into thought.

From Nemerov's point of view the purpose of metaphor is to try to find expression for the inexpressible, for that at least which reason finds inexpressible. In this connection a metaphor may involve not only the novel striking of a relationship between two things which are already known, but may as well encompass a relationship between a known and an unknown thing. In this sense metaphor paradisiacally overcomes not only the separateness of things, or of things and the mind, but strives for a reconciliation between time and eternity. This view contributes to what Nemerov sees informally as the essentially religious nature of art. Art does not beautify an ugly world, but through its marvelous command of form illuminates the inner radiance of objects interfused with mind and thereby generates and celebrates the feeling of being itself. This at least is how he perceives art in his most elevated moods. With characteristic, countervailing vision, however, he has pictured the marvelous edifice of Western art as devolving toward the end of a major phase. Whatever art will look like in the future, he has noted with equanimity, "we will have changed our ways of using words, so that thinking will no longer mean what it did."[48]

CHAPTER 2

The Fiction

I The Short Stories

NEMEROV has published two volumes of short stories, *A Commodity of Dreams* (1959) and *Stories, Fables & Other Diversions* (1971). *A Commodity of Dreams* takes its theme from its title story. Exhibiting Nemerov's penchant for fable, the story is set in an English forest where a man has constructed a museum in which his dreams are carefully cataloged and in which objects that have appeared in his dreams are displayed. The museum is a way of preserving Captain Lastwyn's psychic past as well as tangible articles from his undistinguished life: " 'The little boys and girls, my home, the way we used to live, the little things which happened that one doesn't remember. I've had them all back, I have them all back'. 'Here?' I asked, indicating the files. 'Here, and inside me.' He bowed his head a little, and added, 'I have seen my father smile again, and spoken to my mother—though we said only silly things.' As he raised his head I was not surprised to see tears in his eyes" (p. 64).[1] Captain Lastwyn confides that he is not interested in psychoanalysis, presumably because it would be both superfluous and a semiabstract entry into a subconscious world which presents itself to him with perfect clarity and picturesqueness.

With characteristic poise Nemerov ends the story with the narrator somewhat dazedly taking his leave of the forest museum and boarding a bus which is going in the wrong direction. Rather than get off, he submits to his situation with a newfound quietude. Nemerov's short stories, like those of many contemporary writers, tend to end enigmatically. The jarring effect of these endings is in accord with his belief that, instead of judging the artist's work in the light of their own experience, readers should be encouraged to judge their experience in the light of the artist's work. Knowing that

29

he is regarded as eccentric by the bus conductor, the narrator of "A Commodity of Dreams" placidly conceives of her and of all men as equally, if not knowingly, dreamers, a blurring of the distinction between inner and outer worlds which has Nemerov's deepest assent. The story reveals itself finally as about the drollness and oddity of man's solipsistic infatuation with himself and as such is typical of all of the stories in the collection.

"Yore" offers an analogous tale on a larger scale in which not only individuals but whole communities indulge in solipsism. The scene is the significantly named Forgeterie in the Hotel Beauldvoir and involves a group of worldly cosmopolitans of the sort who inhabited European watering spots at the turn of the century. The conventions of this group include arranged marriages and comfortable harbors, where they can sit out interruptions like war with a feeling of aloof security. Overseen by a bone-china moon, the inhabitants of the Forgeterie ritualistically cultivate the sense of their ordered past against the backdrop of a looming external world whose abrasiveness they will do everything in their power to avoid.

The story centers on Felicia Drum, who has been persuaded to marry an aristocrat whom she does not love. Her outlook is exquisitely bitter. She feels herself caught between two unappealing alternatives—a raw, fearful external world that she knows nothing about and the smoothly ordered and airless world that she does know. She marries as is expected of her, and thereby commits herself to a life of spiritual asphyxiation. This is dramatized in the Wagnerian water opera that she watches, which appears to have been loosely modelled on Andersen's fairy tale "The Little Mermaid." Drifting mentally through the opera, she glows with consciousness as the final grisly scene is played out following the prince's ardent leap into the water to join his mermaid sweetheart for ever:

Felicia was quite in time to see that she, her long white arms fixed firmly around her lover's middle, her silver tail flashing in one powerful turn and dive, dragged him away below. The audience, leaning over the edge of the pool, had a clear view of his silent writhings, kickings and strugglings, accompanied by chains of bubbles from the air in his clothing and one final chain of bubbles from the air in his lungs; after this—it had taken over a minute—he lay still at the entrance of the coral castle, until presently a cortege of mermaids swam down and carried him away, while on distant pianos empty octaves bounded angrily up and down their deserted, echoing stairwells. (p. 12)

The water world with its choreographed violence symbolizes the stifling urbanity exhibited by all of the characters in "Yore." Stylistically, the scene is typical of the way in which Nemerov maintains a fine edge throughout the stories in this collection by counterpointing the note of violence with dry, elegant language and a tragicomic tone.

"Yore" concludes with the echoes of a real war heard in the distant background. Thinking about this war and with conscious irony, Felicia declares finally that "if there's anything in the world I love, it's reality" (p. 13). The statement expresses the stasis that is the configuration of her life. War would at least sweep away the decay that surrounds her and is thus a romantic force in her imagination. She accepts as desolately real on the other hand the outmoded conventions of her social caste and in a sense her final ironic comment with its jadedly self-conscious overtones is an anticlimactic confirmation of her place in that caste.

"The Sorcerer's Eye" is one of a number of stories in *A Commodity of Dreams* which develop the theme of obsessiveness. The story employs a fairy tale motif that includes a forest, castle and beautiful maiden. The girl's father is given the role of the tyrannous giant-God figure who must be overcome—in the best tradition of Freudian fairy tales—if the children are to assume control over their own lives. The glass eye of the tyrannous father, the eye of knowledge, becomes the center of the narrator's obsession. He finally seizes the eye and instantaneously discovers the refined anguish of new awareness. He knows suddenly all of the fear that in childhood "had been denied, all the fear, I think, of children all over the world when in their sinfulness and shame they stand before the mighty parents whom they are bidden to destroy" (p. 244). As a confirmation of the perils of mature vision the beautiful girl who flees with the narrator becomes suddenly transformed into a "thickened, sallow, blotched creature dressed in a somewhat elegant gown which was, however, badly ripped and stained" (p. 243).

The obsessions of Nemerov's unheroic protagonists frequently begin with some small nagging irritant. Sometimes this takes a physical shape, as in "The Twitch," an amusing tale about a self-disciplined Hollywood mogul who has weathered a lifetime of anti-Semitism and a young Aryan actor who, reacting subconsciously to his own racism, twitches uncontrollably in having to play the part of a Jew. In "The Guilty Shall Be Found Out and Punished" the narrator is obsessed with an elusive itch under his right foot which he cannot understand but which the reader associates with lascivious impulses that the narrator is too timid to express but about which he still feels vaguely guilty. The guilt is a sign of the cultural and social origins of many of the characters' obsessions. The obsession of the protagonist in "The Web of Life" originates in a social convention, that of respect for the dead. He is condemned to see both his own life and his inheritance slowly evaporate in preserving his dead great uncle in an expensive cryogenic mechanism that is designed to provide the old man with a fresh-frozen immortality. Bound to his great uncle's posthumous obsession by the conditions of inheritance, the narrator acknowledges with chagrin the oddity of his simultaneously fortunate and helpless position: "If Great-uncle taught me one thing for which I am thankful, it is that money is the blood of the world, and as things are now I can comfortably go on bleeding for years, for life." (p. 87). The theme of man's powerlessness is pointed up repeatedly in these stories of obsession—a powerlessness which like that depicted in "The Web of Life" frequently lurks within the very trappings of power.

Nemerov had intended to call his first book of stories *Obsessions*, only later changing the title to *A Commodity of Dreams*. The appropriateness of the original title is evident throughout the book. In "Tradition" the principal character funnels his life into the slaughtering of thousands of crows, taking advantage of a forgotten village bounty on crows. He then creates a marginal handicraft industry out of the bones and feathers of dead crows and creates a legend about the massacre of the crows by inventing a plague of crows and some heroic ancestors to deal with them. Infuriated by him at first, the town finally honors his death as a member of one of the area's oldest families. In addition to dramatizing one man's obsession, the story embodies a conspicuous Nemerovian theme, that of the impact of imagination on external reality.

At the same time the obsessed characters generally find themselves at some point, often a point of no return, in collision with the external world. Such is the case with Samuel Amran in "An Encounter with the Law." Amran drives north from New York City in the autumn to see the New England foliage, his powder-blue Cadillac gliding effortlessly through the tiny white villages. He relaxes as he feels the weight of commercial and familial responsibility sliding from his shoulders. Unthinkingly he flicks a cigar butt out of the car window which suddenly brings him face to face with a humorless policeman who becomes the incarnation of his most surrealistic fears: "Except for mouth and chin, the man seemed to have no face but to be all blue-gray cloth, black leather and green glass; even his skin was leathery, red, rough, and his peeling nose seemed to incorporate itself somehow with the sunglasses which in turn fitted closely, concealingly, under the visor of his cap. He wore great black gauntlets going nearly to the elbows, and his belt sagged to one side under the weight of the holstered gun" (pp. 204 - 05).

Humiliated and flustered, Amran tries to bribe the policeman, who in turn orders him to go to the police station. Following the policeman's motorcycle, Amran comes to a fork in the road, a location that seems to flow from an earlier dream and he goes berserk, gunning the engine in a frantic attempt to escape. Exhilarated and flushed with a sense of power, Amran forges through what has become a solipsistic experience only to find that there are unforeseen, real consequences ahead as he smashes into the policeman, killing him instantly. He returns to contact with the external world with a heavy sadness, taking off the policeman's cap and sunglasses and noticing that the "face beneath was younger, softer, than what he had expected" (p. 210). The obsessions of characters like Amran are manifestations in Nemerov's short story typology of the impasse between the mind and the external world, an impasse whose consequences are as catastrophic as they are unavoidable.

While obsession leads to disaster in colliding with the external world, the energy which brings about the catastrophe generally comes from within, a satisfying circumstance in stories which focus in any case on characterization. This can be seen in "Delayed Hearing" in which a car accident so infuriates one of the victims, Miss Mindenhart, that she pursues the other driver with mounting fury through the courts. Frustrated by the inability of the courts to bend to her will, Miss Mindenhart strikes out at her gentle, pacifistic adversary in a scene that brings about the woman's surprising death and registers Nemerov's sense of the human condition:

If Mr. Julius Porter had not grabbed at his cousin's arm, slightly deflecting the trajectory of the handbag; if Mrs. Haxton had only put up an arm to ward off the blow, as Miss Minderhart assuredly anticipated she must do . . . if only Mrs. Haxton had not at this moment confirmed herself in a religion of suffering nonresistance; if only, above all, she had not worn that smile . . . But as it was, the silver- or chrome-plated arrow of the handbag pierced her left eye, and there was a grotesque instant of silence and motion arrested everywhere (p. 199).

With detachment and irony Nemerov shows the inevitable coming together of the willful and the inexorable in a pattern of determination so far reaching and so pervasive that it is identical in a diffused state with the very atmosphere of his fictional world.

An excruciating tale of obsession is "The Amateurs." The title plays on the Latin word for love—a contrast with the bored group of elegant sado-masochists whose obsessive tormenting of one another results in the crucifixion of one of its members. Osmin, the man who is crucified, draws a romantic named Allan Hastings into carrying out the crucifixion by playing on the need of Hastings and the group for some conclusive *action*. The action performed is intended by Osmin to satisfy both Hastings's need for finality and the group's perverse hunger for raw emotional experience. The crucifixion serves the purpose of freeing Osmin from the prolonged self-hatred that has constituted his life. Fittingly, his death effects its intended catharsis as Hastings, overcome by what has happened, breaks into a "deep, healthy laughter" (p. 183). The story firmly underlines the fact that Nemerov's characters will what they are compelled to will even when they are completely aware of the brutal mechanism underlying their lives.

The propensity of the characters for violence when they are separated subjectively from the world around them is dramatized in the story "A Secret Society." Judson Paley, a New England aristocrat, is both socially and psychologically cut off from the town in which he lives. Ostensibly enjoying the idle life of privilege, Paley in fact seethes with a helpless feeling of violence and alienation. Steeped in self-consciousness, he moves about town under the pressure of strange impulses. On one occasion he is driven by the temptation to take a policeman's revolver and kill himself. He finally does seize a bank guard's gun and turns it on himself, but he forgets to release the safety catch. A failure even in this, he is carried back home, whimpering.

The guard's gun becomes an obsessive symbol of Paley's desire to have some sort of impact on the world around him, a contrast with his pampered and ineffectual existence. Holding the gun in his hand, he feels that he holds the "absolute upon which everything was founded, the black imperative whose existence made conditional the existence of everything else, the banks, schools, stores, theaters; waitresses, barbers, dentists and hygienists too, for that matter; himself as well, come to that" (p. 33). Nemerov's characterization of Judson Paley is characteristic of his technique in *A*

Commodity of Dreams in that it combines the luridness of the violent and the grotesque with the blandness of the mundane. He opens "A Secret Society" with a description of Paley in the barber's chair, a scene which is uncomfortably self-conscious for Paley but which makes the reader aware of the ordinary world that goes its way outside the membrane of Paley's obsessions.

An occasional character will strive to break down the impasse between himself and the external world, sometimes wittily, as in the story "Beyond the Screen." In the 1950s, when not everyone had a television set and not everyone wanted one, Andrew Stonecroft has his house invaded by his mother-in-law and her TV. The world relayed through the set becomes for Stonecroft an emblem of the solipsism of his whole society, which attunes itself to reality only within the abstract, cinematic shadows of the living room screen. As Stonecroft watches the parade of real deaths which constitutes the world's news pass narcotically across the screen, he decides to act. In the midst of a thunderstorm he rips out the lightning arrester from behind his house, determined to take his chances with life and death along with those unfortunates on the TV news, most of them in the developing nations, whose lives still have some extra subjective reality.

All of the stories in *A Commodity of Dreams* possess a firm symmetry, a feature of Nemerov's narrative style. The most symmetrical is probably the story "The Ocean to Cynthia," which involves a charming confidence man, Anthony Bower, who has spent his life seducing and living off well-to-do women he meets on transatlantic liners. Bower typifies Nemerov's attraction to stories which have to do with fraud: "Debasement and counterfeit especially of the intellectual and artistic currency," he wrote on one occasion, constitute a "subject of great charm."[2] Flanking Anthony Bower is Father Frank, a fake priest who is anything but frank, and Elizabeth Brayle whose name symbolizes her blindness to Bower's designs.

The denouement comes when Bower is shocked to discover, through a locket containing a love inscription he had written many years before, that the woman he is now attempting to seduce is his own daughter, the illegitimate offspring of an earlier seduction. Swept away by an unusual wave of recognition and despair, he hurls both himself and Elizabeth into the sea with a final flourish so that they move together "as though dancing toward the free fall and the wild marble water singing below" (p. 103). As the passage illustrates and as is the case with most of these stories, the tight symmetry of the plot is matched by the chiselled precision and grace of Nemerov's prose.

On the whole *Stories, Fables & Other Diversions* (1971) is a more formal and subdued collection than *A Commodity of Dreams*. Although it contains some memorable tales, it tends to lack the dramatic energy of the earlier volume. The antiheroic qualities of the protagonists in *Stories, Fables & Other Diversions* are even more pronounced than in *A Commodity of Dreams* and the writing sometimes has a flatness that tends to undermine the dramatic potential of the stories. The characters are as alienated as in *A Commodity of Dreams* and Nemerov's view of them is as wry as ever. The reader is led to be even more detached from them than in *A Commodity of Dreams* and is moved to identify with the metaphysical condition of the characters rather than with their personal traits and circumstances. This is largely due to the emphasis on fable, a form which Nemerov values for its conciseness.

In addition, although they are still driven by subconscious forces, the characters in *Stories, Fables & Other Diversions* are more self-contained than those in the earlier collection. The narrator of the story "Unbelievable Characters," for example, longs for a violence which does not appear. Watching a skywriting plane spell the syllable "ROB-," he wonders if the completed instruction will be "ROB—BURN—MURDER." The word turns out to be "ROBIN," a word sadly bereft of dramatic connotations. Bored to the limit, he concludes finally that there was always the "millionth chance" that the smoking plane was "really on fire, that the smoke would turn black and begin to plunge away down the sky" (pp. 36 - 37).[3] The scene reflects an idle interest in violence in a dessicated world rather than the bursting of violence from beneath and within that marks the lives of those in *A Commodity of Dreams*.

The characters in *Stories, Fables & Other Diversions* are devotees of consciousness. Even Mrs. Melisma in "Bon Bons," who has a craving for filled chocolates, becomes a practitioner of self-analysis, the "passionate scientist of her vice" (p. 28). Hoisted up by Nemerov as an emblem of North American materialism, Mrs. Melisma pores over her dilemma: "She saw that life had embarked her on a hopeless quest for the One Supreme filled chocolate, containing in itself not the abstract or mere quintessence but the entire luscious being of the absolute; in the search for which all actual experience fell into the gullet and abyss of non-being, and was as nothing. Nor would the Platonic Idea of that chocolate satisfy; no, it must be the real thing, the filled chocolate incarnate, and to eat it would be to redeem time" (p. 28). The passage reveals the strength of *Stories, Fables & Other Diversions,* its nimble play of mind and language, bringing the collection into line with Nemerov's lyric poetry, so that what the stories lack in action they make up in the refined elaboration of idea. The narrative style is carefully distilled, with plots that are firmly contained and coolly ordered.

All of these qualities can be found in "The Nature of the Task," one of the strongest stories in the collection. The story is a Kafkaesque fable in which a man named Palen is given the task of killing flies in a square-shaped room. There is no indication of who has given him this task, but it would seem that he has been dealt the assignment by God or life and that he has accepted it. Not noticing any flies, his mind, which is in constant need of stimulation, seizes upon the idea of counting snowflakes. Remembering that he once heard that to count things was to kill them, he equates the counting of snowflakes with the killing of flies. He starts by counting the blue snowflakes on the walls of his room and then switches to counting snowflakes falling outside. He becomes blocked finally by the thought that since no two snowflakes are alike he may not in fact be counting identical objects. In stopping his counting, he suddenly becomes conscious of a fly buzzing in the room, a fly which had presumably been there all along but which he only became aware of when he stepped outside the confinement of his own mind.

As in "Bon Bons" Nemerov embellishes the story with metaphysical witticisms. He satirizes religious consolation, for example, in a scene showing Palen's scruples about carrying out his task: "One must simply sit still. Indeed, that might be precisely the mystical import of an instruction to kill the flies in a room where no flies were: that is, do nothing—the chief recommendation of the great religious of every persuasion from the beginning of the world" (p. 104). The story goes deeper than its verbal wit, however. Palen does not hastily confuse mind with world; rather, he is led to recognize the precociousness of consciousness in extracting meaning from a world which holds its meaning to itself. The rage for order is inevitable, however, given the mere existence of the mind. This is signified in the way in which Palen divides even the barred window into an intelligible grid, like that of a chessboard, so that the "sky, the single tree, the passing cloud, even the occasional bird, appeared superimposed on a graph" (p. 96). Reaching a plateau of Nemerovian wisdom, Palen stoically accepts his own inventiveness as the "glibness of a mind that moved, it seemed, independently of his will," and he comes finally to a "deep and thoroughgoing distrust of the reason—just because it 'reasoned' so very well" (p. 103).

While Palen arrives at a healthy skepticism, other characters in *Stories, Fables & Other Diversions* lack his perspective. "The Idea of a University" was titled after Cardinal Newman's celebrated discourse on the purpose of a university and is a satiric sketch about intelligence isolated from the world around it. For Newman a university was a place for intellectual and moral formation, and he would have had little sympathy with the university in Nemerov's story, which seems to be an appendage of American technology. Furthermore, the moral status of Nemerov's fictional campus is silhouetted in the university's establishing its own slum for interdisciplinary study, a slum composed of poor people who had been imported from Georgia. The slum symbolizes the arrogance of the mind as well as the potential destructiveness of intelligence when it is abstractly detached from matter and from the external world. While far from being a social commentator, Nemerov has frequently underlined the severe social ramifications of intellectual aloofness.

Nemerov's contemporary university develops in piecemeal fashion, adding an aircraft hangar here, an experimental prison unit there. It develops sporadically and mindlessly into a receptacle for random spillovers from the larger society instead of providing that society with clarification and direction about its fundamental nature and purposes. The impotency of the academic community is illustrated in the scene in which the president of the university is peremptorily denied entrance to the experimental prison which is ostensibly part of his domain but which is actually controlled by the Pentagon. The meaning of this scene is amplified in the conclusion of the sketch, which focuses on the brain of the university, the significantly named Random Access Computer Unit. Inside the building that isolates the computer from the community it is meant to serve, a large typewriter "with no evidence of human control or for that matter attention" is seen "patiently printing something across and down an apparently endless roll of paper that fed in turn into a large but overflowing wastebasket" (p. 95).

A number of the tales in *Stories, Fables & Other Diversions* show Nemerov's interest in fantasy. Examples include "The Twelve and the One," "The Outage," "The Executive," and "The Nature of the Task." Of these the most imaginative and powerful is "The

Executive," a story about an encounter between the white manager of a supermarket, Mr. Budby, and Hubert, his black stock boy. Hubert is a walking disaster who innocently but effectively destroys whatever he comes into contact with. On one occasion, for example, he thoughtlessly leaves hundreds of cartons of fish standing out in the June sun. The manager, who enjoys thinking of himself as an executive, is a churchgoer whose anger over the costly ineptitude of his stock boy is tempered by moral scruples as well as by the store's policy of racial integration.

Nevertheless, Budby finds himself on the brink of firing his employee when he suddenly has a vision of Hubert transfigured into a luminous black angel: "The brightness circling his head hissed and crackled against the ceiling, but did not seem to set it aflame. Dark, downy wings stood out of Hubert's back, and fluttered a bit wildly, maybe because Hubert was still trembling some. Hubert's eyes, behind their limpid brown, flamed like stars, bending upon Mr. Budby an icy radiance" (p. 22). Budby keeps waiting for Hubert to become a proper angel with pink skin, fair hair and blue eyes, but all that happens is that a "blaze of black light, a blazing blackness like the moonlit glimpse of calm waters, continued to glimmer all around Hubert" (p. 22).

The intensity of the vision casts a spell over the relationship between Budby and Hubert for a while, but then as the feeling of the vision wears off and Hubert continues to blunder through the week, the manager gathers himself to act in spite of the scorched arc which he perceives nervously on the ceiling. In a final denial of the vision to which, after all, there had been no witnesses, he fires Hubert. "The Executive," is the most dramatic of the stories in *Stories, Fables & Other Diversions* and is executed with finesse and economy. An urbane tone hovers over the narration, but it is modulated carefully so that it diminishes in the sections in which the characters' consciousnesses are the center of interest. Through such subtle alterations in tone, texture and mood, all of which contribute to the unity of effect, Nemerov demonstrates, here as elsewhere, his polished mastery of the short story.

II   The Melodramatists

Nemerov's first published novel, *The Melodramatists* (1949), was written during three successive summers. The last sixty pages, which comprise the denouement, were written in a creative cloudburst, two fifteen-hour sessions preceded by "(a) a mean quarrel with a friend, and (b) a month during which I did nothing but (of all things) play golf."[4] The novel is set in Boston in the winter of 1940 and involves the Boynes, a family of Boston Brahmins whose elder members try vainly to maintain appearances. The Boyne parents begin the action in an attempt to impose their values, specifically about marriage and divorce, upon their children. They only partly succeed. The insipid nature of their success in calling off the divorce of their son Roger and his wife Leonora is registered by Mr. Boyne, who perceives all of life as essentially a struggle for power:

The elders . . . had won, there would be no divorce. But they too realized that something had been sacrificed. They had been presented with a puppet performance, cheated of the life. Among the random images that went through Nicholas Boyne's mind was one of some Roman general who had ordered the execution of his own son on a battlefield; and another, more vaguely recalled, of a Roman—was it ambassador?—who for some reason had stuck his hand in a pot of fire and seen it consumed. To prove something, was it? (p. 34)[5]

Having failed to achieve a satisfying victory, Mr. Boyne obligingly goes mad and thereby hands over the reins to the next generation. The daughters Susan and Claire dominate the action, with the plot revolving around their experiments with life. Susan explores the world of earthly love while Claire devotes herself to asceticism and mysticism. Both assume that they can fashion for themselves whatever lives their minds can imagine and much of the satire has to do with the collision between this adventurousness and the obstinate external world. Susan finds herself, for example, being blackmailed by her butler, Hogan, for indiscretions involving Dr. Einman and the family treasury; whereas Claire finds herself saddled with a group of smelly Hungarian nuns and eventually in the power of a prostitute, who has the appropriate name of Mother Fosker. So much, the plot seems to say, for the free exploration of life.

Nemerov's fondness for symmetry is seen in the careful way in which he parallels the lives of the two women. Upon the collapse of their father, for example, each quickly sets her own course. Susan becomes Dr. Einman's mistress on the same evening and in the same house in which Claire places her soul trustingly into the pastoral care of Father Meretruce. Even at twenty-one, when Claire was two years older than her sister, she had developed a "spinsterish asperity of voice and, on occasion, the primness of a young dowager" (p. 27). She approaches experience, particularly of the flesh, with fear and loathing: "Why can't we keep our lives clean?" she complains to Susan on one occasion. "Why is there this perpetual making of dirty jokes running like a sound-track beside us, as though some—some horrible little toadstools were leaning together and whispering about us?" Unsatisfied with her sister's inconclusive response, she moves to the window, where she thrills at the "wonderful coldness," her mind filled with "images of coldness, of the magnificent vaulted solemnity of churches; convents, white stiff robes, coldness, centuries cold as the tomb devoted to denouncing warmth, intimacy" (p. 29).

Claire's frigidity, so incisively described in this passage, is complemented by a burning zeal for the spiritual. Under the guiding hand of Father Meretruce she embraces mystical asceticism like a lover, climbing eagerly to visionary heights. Taking pain as an ally, she clenches herself in prayerful anticipation of mystical union and experiences with full empathy the vision of Christ on the cross. Restraining the novel's prevailing tone of skepticism at this critical moment, Nemerov focuses eloquently on the expanding circles of Claire's ecstasy:

it was the instantaneous spread of light in the center of her mind, together with impressions of tremendous majesty, a light so white and blinding that our earthly robes seemed by contrast tarred and defiled. In agony and love she saw this light glitter and gleam in brilliant flashes through her spine and head, unbearable in intensity, so that she wished and did not wish for the end. The light like thunder echoed in the circle of her mind, played in fitful coruscations among the gray, coiling masses of her brain, so that she seemed to see by flashes of utter radiance her own essence, that which slept and that which waked, its purities and its corruptions, the carbon and the many-faceted diamond. (p. 127)

Claire's mystical ecstasy exists in lieu of a strong faith, a fact which becomes uncomfortably apparent when the officious Father Meretruce, a visionless man himself, casts doubt upon the authenticity of her experience. Further complicating her assent to Catholic dogma is the arrival of the unkempt, monolingual Hungarian nuns whose physical unattractiveness awakens her queasiness. Staring at the salivating nuns who are caught up stupefyingly in their mumbled prayers, she wavers between seeing them as merely bestial or as living in "the skull of God" (p. 224).

Uncertain and yet eager to believe, she fears finally that the fury of the nuns' praying may after all be merely their obsession, a narrowing of the variety and sanity of the many forms of reality to the "nonsense of the One" (p. 224). Nevertheless, she forces herself to be receptive to the visitation of God, only to have appear instead "the towers of Notre Dame de Paris—pigeons in the sunlight of a public square—some sort of tall monument with a figure on its top." Where, she wonders, were the "well-known peace and the much-advertised consolation?" (p. 253). Repressed almost to the last, Claire finally drifts subconsciously toward sexual union with Edmond Einman while upholding her conscious distaste for the body and for human love: "The idea of love revolted her; it was unclean" (p. 281).

In spite of his clear reservations about her, Nemerov invests Claire with intelligence and the capacity to grow. She eventually confronts the flesh in the shape of Mother Fosker and her cohort of allegedly reformed prostitutes. The confrontation produces in Claire a perception of the relationship between religion and subconscious sexuality which is sophisticated, if a trifle glib, and which eventually helps to free her: "She imagined that many must have witnessed with hot pleasure the Son of Man writhing on the Cross, which pleasure might in some subterranean change after his death have been the motive of their conversion. They feared, perhaps, the vengeance of the dead, not because they had killed Him but because He bore away into death the deepest powers of their lust" (p. 281). Like the other characters Claire is a melodramatist, brooding bitterly over her own unhappiness and that of others in a way that is simultaneously both moving and lugubrious: "To be unhappy, that is the weakness fullest of shame; that we are unhappy is the thing we dread most to be told, unless we dread still more the idea that another can think us unhappy" (p. 259). As with a number of the characters Claire's sentiments are a shade too ponderous and uncompromising.

From a structural point of view Nemerov divides his novel between the viewpoints of Susan and Claire, leaving some room for the consciousnesses of Einman and a few of the others. Susan receives more narrative time than any of the characters, reflecting Nemerov's interest in and sympathy with her. At the same time, in order to offset the dominance of Susan's viewpoint, he punctuates the flow of her consciousness with some unappealing illuminations of her. In one scene, for example, in which she is with Edmond Einman, she throws an unattractive light upon herself in displaying her feelings of boredom by yawning openly: "Edmond's talk, so long as it could be understood as primarily attacking her virtue and only in the second place sowing information, had been acceptable enough, a flattering attention. Now, however, it became a bore" (p. 119).

Symmetrically, Susan's dark hair and shapeliness contrast with Claire's fairness and angularlity. Intellectually as well she is different from her sister. Impatiently on one occasion she complains about Claire's "perpetual mooning about noble motives" (p. 28). As with Claire, though, the Boyne affluence provides Susan with an opportunity to explore herself and what life has to offer, an adventure which is given thrust by the sudden, shocking collapse of her father's mind, a reminder that time is change and a melancholy indication of life's "infinite capriciousness" (p. 115). Nevertheless, Mr. Boyne's plunge into dementia sharpens Susan's appetite for life so that what she wants it to contain is a sense of "crisis, passion, decision, fulfilment" (p. 115).

Susan's approach to new experience is much less methodical than Claire's and her goals less clearly defined. She confides to Claire on one occasion that she can find out what her goals are only by wanting something first. Her plight is that her gravitating toward passion and finality collides with the "triviality and absurdity of things" (p. 202). Edmond Einman, to whom Susan becomes fatefully attached, is the spokesman for the triviality and absurdity of things, a philosophy of life that Susan cannot gainsay and that she seems to use subconsciously as an intellectual support for her drifting toward an amoral sensuality. Thus Einman becomes both her lover and the nihilistic underminer of the passion that she shares with him, a situation that presents itself to her as a bitter paradox: "She found his sexual powers more satisfying now in bitterness than previously in amusement, and his fancy in this matter more varied and provocative: the savage gratifications they achieved, though occasionally, and not without a mute anger liable at any moment to petty and spiteful fulmination, were the landmarks to bring into momentary focus the desolate plain on which she was" (p. 202).

Susan's commitment to love becomes indistinguishable from her commitment to death. Her conception of love, the product of a sensitive and imaginative mind, reflects this antithetical range of feeling: "Passion, tenderness, pity—she saw in her mind a spider scuttling on a wall—were suicidal extravagances of the will, the image of whose desire was really the white silence of the hospital room, the cool sheets, the bloodless redress of these grievances. And love (as one reverently called it, the very syllable a breath, an apologetic sigh, of weariness) tended that same way too" (p. 213).

Susan's viewpoint is so complexly persuasive that she gives the appearance of being the one character who is exempt from being a melodramatist. She resents Claire's "gushing," for example, "no less than her assumed familiarity" (pp. 149 - 147). Listening to John Averist declare his love for her, she becomes sardonically aware that every admission was a "place of concealment for some further secret," open sincerity a sure sign of "vile deceit" (p. 151). Slumming through Boston in the company of Einman, she decides finally that the smell of beer and urinals was the only significant difference between the city's low life and her own sphere. On another occasion she notices a garishly dressed woman whom she takes to be a whore and following her out of curiosity has the "inconclusive pleasure of seeing her enter a respectable-looking brownstone house on Beacon Street" (p. 95).

Critical and shrewd, Susan does fathom her entanglement with Einman. If it is true that she cannot help herself, it is equally true that she avoids self-pity. She accepts the perversity of her relationship with him, a relationship whose "melancholy charm lay in disillusion which when it could not provoke it would invent" (p. 214). Furthermore, she confronts the ugliness of her life with courage. Scrutinizing one of the reformed whores whom Claire has admitted to the Boyne mansion, she becomes aware of a "loathsome softness" which causes her to bow her head in recognition: "I too am like that, she thought" (p. 264).

In desiring passion and finality, however, Susan is a melodramatist. She is also a melodramatist in resolving the relationship with Einman in a pact of mutual abnegation, a pact which he cunningly engineers by making her believe that he is terminally ill, a stratagem that he calculates will alter her course from death to that of renunciation. A melodramatist in taking the bait, she tells Einman, whom she considers near his end, that they will be a "Christian household, forgiving each other daily for everything" (p. 216). Ironically, Susan exhibits a religious tenderness at this moment which seems forever beyond Claire's reach. She is a melodramatist finally, however, in assuming that what she decides will determine her life, a mistake made by all of the major characters. It is, after all, Mother Fosker and Hogan, emissaries of the intractable outer world, who are the final shapers of her fate.

Even Edmond Einman, who promenades through the pages of the novel as the ultimate realist, is a melodramatist. Einman's nihilism, the venom of which he injects into his relationship with Susan, is based upon a solipsistic despair which is only partially alleviated by the relief which he finds in cerebration. Einman's philosophical perorations are the refreshment of his soul, particularly when communicated to an attentive audience, such as that at the party at which Arthur Charvet attempts to kill himself. Using the incident as his point of departure, Einman quickly moves onto more generalized reflections:

The definition, the essence, of life, look, is this: not that it moves, no. But that it continues to move, it keeps going—so far as we can see, at any rate; though we must never overlook the possibility, the rarest joke of all, that what we live in is not life at all, but simply the vast motion of a mechanical energy to the largest scale, like a rock falling from the highest mountain, like a ship—with its gods and emperors, crew and passengers, its fine foods and economic problems—sinking slowly down the height of an incredibly deep ocean. (p. 55)

Although Einman touches on some metaphysical ideas that resemble aspects of Nemerov's thinking, he does so with a pedagogical gravity that Nemerov clearly satirizes. Furthermore, Einman's confidence in thought, his ingenuous assumption that his philosophizing about the futility of life has any impact on the course of things, is his most melodramatic illusion. It is the most fundamental mistake that a Nemerovian character can make and is probably as close as Nemerov ever came to depicting tragic *hubris*.

The denouement of *The Melodramatists* has the dramatic flair of Restoration comedy. The final confrontation scene, which assembles all of the central characters, also reflects Nemerov's passion for the detective story. The Boyne mansion becomes a tableau of the whole society with the privileged and powerful in revelry below while those who represent intellect and spirit are held prisoner in the upper part of the house. In a burlesque of institutionalized religion, Mother Fosker, with her pulse on the outer world, oversees everything like a demanding Mother Superior.

In spite of their ineffectualness those who represent mind and spirit are the focus of narrative attention since they are more interesting even in failure than their Saturnalian counterparts below. The upper room is the repository of culture, a museum of philosophy and religion. The scene represents a culmination of the past for the characters as well. Susan ruefully acknowledges this when she considers that "one forgot nothing; everything that had happened was there, was still there, and not dead either, but alive and mysteriously moving, the crawling corruption of the past by which one bred the future" (p. 316). Part of the action involves a debate between Dr. Einman and Father Meretruce on science and religion. The debate is as inconclusive as it is meaningless and irrelevant to the representatives of the active world in the rooms below them. Neither Dr. Einman nor Father Meretruce present a convincing case for either science or religion. One of the reasons for this is that Nemerov does not want to turn his novel over to discussion. The points of view expressed by the debaters are merely colors on the novelist's palette and are meant to engage the characters and the reader rather than to elucidate the human condition.

The fact that the debate focuses eventually on the topic of love is not only a source of great irony among such acerbic and disillusioned protagonists, but is in fact unexpectedly relevant. Each of their conceptions of love, both human and divine, together with the machinations and complications attendant upon these conceptions has led, at least in part, to the bizarre spectacle of Hogan holding them all prisoner in an upstairs room. Claire recognizes all of this when she exclaims toward the end: "I am shut in a room in my own house and watched by a man with a pistol—simply because of love and its mysterious ways" (p. 328).

The death of Susan is carefully and ambiguously described by Nemerov so that it is seen simultaneously as the ultimate expression of power by Hogan and as suicide, Susan's earlier submission to Hogan having filled her with a final, despairing self-revulsion. Her death is at once pathetic and absurd. It captures the novel's complex mood—its melancholy, poignancy, and ludicrousness. The mood is sharpened at the end by the elegant surface of the action being ruptured by violence. The complex mood represents Nemerov's bifocal view of fate closing in on man, a fate that registers both the meaninglessness of life and the surprisingly fixed laws of character and behavior that lead relentlessly to unforeseen destruction. The denouement of *The Melodramatists* may be compared to the laws that Nemerov perceived underlying the ending of Faulkner's *Light in August:* "Event ineluctably creates event, there is no escape from the assigned role, the idea of freedom consists in our having forgotten that we learned the part we must play. God, or destiny, or luck, or life itself, is inherently novelistic . . . coincidence itself has no longer any real existence but is unabashedly faced up to as necessity."[6]

With characteristic balance Nemerov follows the death of Susan Boyne with a brief scene of recovery and adaptation. Amidst the relaxed yawning of Father Meretruce, Claire goes over to the harpsichord: "She sat down and began to play, inattentively at first but presently with more care, a little piece in fugue. The instrument was out of tune and not only that, but broken glass tinkled on some of the strings, but it seemed not to matter. The morning light seemed to clear the room as the voices in a minor key steadily moved to and from one another, showing an inexorable confidence in their not quite harmonious world" (p. 338). In spite of the feeling of chaos unleashed by Susan's death, the surface of life closes over again with Claire apparently turning away from religion and toward art in her quest for spiritual meaning. Furthermore, culture, as symbolized by the out-of-tune harpsichord, appears to respond.

The central motif in the novel is that articulated in the title. The melodramatic is mirrored in the names—the name Leonora, for example—and is present in every character in the novel with the exception of Mother Fosker, who symbolizes objective reality. Among the minor characters, John Averist, for example, is a sentimentalist: "It was the habit of his soul to wallow romantically. He was in love with Susan, he thought, and made of what he proposed to himself as a hopeless passion, together with her obvious accessibility at least to another, something rather special in the way of emotion" (p. 141).

Even the imperturbable Hogan slips into a melodramatic frame of mind on occasion, as in the scene in which he faces John Averist in a showdown over Hogan's blackmailing of Susan. Hogan assumes that Averist has come to kill him and reflects histrionically: "You pushed the victim's patience too far, you did not know when to stop, you would be found, one gray dawn, lying with your iron-gray hair in a pool of mud that gradually was becoming red. By your side was the strange oriental weapon—yataghan or kris—that did you in" (p. 190). Similarly, before his collapse, old Mr. Boyne is depicted as melodramatic in standing for what he regards as old-fashion values, all the while exhibiting an "incredibly devious, Machiavellian smile" (p. 25).

While the characters perceive as reality what the reader sees as unreality, the characters perceive as dream what the reader judges to be reality. Averist, for example, cannot accept the reality of his own behavior in trying to decide whether or not to share in the blackmail money that Susan pays to Hogan. He imagines himself transferring the money to Edmond, his rival, so that ironically Edmond might spend the night in a hotel with Susan. The situation becomes ludicrous in its dreamlike illumination of a world "full of connections, circles, cycles and dark designs," a world whose ingrown complexities and accompanying ironies strike Averist as preposterously unreal (p. 198).

Susan Boyne is also susceptible to perceiving the world as a dream. As the allegedly reformed prostitutes arrive at the Boyne mansion in the company of policemen and Father Meretruce, Susan, watching from above, perceives the scene as having a quality of "remote and silent intensity, as though (she thought) it were an advertisement for a dream" (p. 262). Her own life comes to seem to her to be "dangerously dreamlike," a feeling which persists as she contemplates ending that life (p. 200). She "lay down on the bed and held the point of the knife to her side. She had little enough idea where to strike so as to be sure. But the symbolic propriety of the place and the position struck her as contemptible and operatic, so she got up and took the knife into the bathroom, whose white and hygienic brightness she imagined her blood as already soiling" (pp. 316 - 17). The use of the dream motif is Nemerov's way of turning the novel inside out. The melodramatic delusions which fill the subjective lives of the characters but which are unrecognized by them become projected in the outer world as a cosmic parallel for the ever fluctuating margin between the imagined and the real. Much of the novel's narrative apparatus—the unlikely appearance of the Hungarian nuns and the prostitutes in the Boyne mansion, for example—extends the perimeters of the dreamscape to include the reader.

Nemerov uses a technique of surrealistic formalism. The formalism is conveyed through the novel's restraint and urbanity. He admired the dryness of Stendhal, who, when he wrote *The Charterhouse of Parma,* read a page of the *Code Civil* every morning— for the style. *The Melodramatists* centers on a humanized world with only the most perfunctory attention given to nature. In addition, Nemerov circumscribes his characters with epigrams and aphorisms in the manner of Neoclassical writers. Similarly, he

makes liberal use of ironic juxtaposition, a favorite Neoclassical
device, as in the scene in which Susan pays off Hogan each week by
placing forty dollars under the bust of Plato which stands on the
harpsichord in the library.

The formalism is emotionally reinforced by Nemerov's antipathy
to sentimentalism. He summarized his attitude toward sentimentality memorably in the poem "To the Bleeding Hearts Association
of American Novelists": "I like those masters better who ex-
pound/more inwardly the nature of our loss,/ And only offhand let
us know they've found/ No better composition than a cross."[7]

Nemerov also strove to make his plot intricate and formal. He has
been quoted as saying that he does not regard character in the novel
as a very deep matter: "And I certainly do not read fiction to be
told how terrible the world is. I can find that out on the morning
news."[8] His use of the mock-heroic also inhibits the rush of emotion
and emphasizes the formalism of the style. When Hogan is about to
enter Susan's room to claim her, an act that destroys her, Nemerov
offsets the chilling implications of the scene with a mock-heroic
description of the door through which he passes: "Anciently the
guardian of gateways was Janus, whose two faces, though they
gained him a reputation for irony and deceit, were merely the image and denomination, as honest as possible, of the crucial situation
expressed by a door: that it had to do with inside and outside and
represented therefore the entire possibility of human society, which
without this distinction could not have existed" (p. 273).

Hogan is the focus for much of the mock-heroic imagery because
he combines insignificance of soul with a large and calculating ambition. Projecting himself out of his servitude into the upper classes,
he lives out the melodrama of his life in the imagined company of
kings and generals:

According to the paradigm of history, as Hogan understood it, the Boyne
household was passing through a period of decadence, an interregnum con-
sequent on the abdication of the supreme authority (Mr and Mrs Boyne),
the over-running of the domain by barbarians (whores and nuns), the dis-
pute over the throne between two princesses, of whom one was swayed by
the Church and the other was accessible to lust: the erotic and the political
were in conjunction and in favorable aspect, and Hogan's star was at last,
by some means not entirely clear, to rise. (p. 270)

The pervasive use of the mock-heroic enters the realm of reflexiveness when Nemerov enters the narration with derisive

philosophical conceits of his own, as in his description of Charvet's attempted suicide: "The party had rather rapidly changed its quality. The proximate cause of the change was evidently alcohol. The formal cause was Arthur Charvet, and the material cause lay perhaps far back and forgotten, somewhere in the tangled mess of relations in space and time that was so glibly referred to as Arthur Charvet. The final cause, however, seemed to be Dr. Einman" (p. 47). The effect of the scene is to place Nemerov as narrator between his characters and the reader and thus to prevent the reader's sympathetic identification with the characters. The technique is necessary in order to sustain the hybrid tragicomic perspective.

The symbolism in the novel is also of a rather formal order. Similes abound and there is overt symbolic use made of setting in the case of the Boyne mansion. The house, which symbolizes the withered vitality of Western civilization, is built around an "enclosed court" which is "stone-flagged and bordered by arched columns; in its center stood a fountain that did not work" (p. 293). The most elaborate and insistent symbol is the photograph of the fetus which Einman carries around with him. The arms of the fetus are folded in "judicial and almost contemptuous posture," and the mouth, similarly, seems "cruel and royal and full of sullen condemnation" (p. 80). The photograph becomes an absorbing talisman for Susan, who accepts it as an emblem of the alien and enigmatic world outside the mind and the self.

The Melodramatists is not as evenly polished a structure as Nemerov's second novel *Federigo*. It has a looseness, for example, that becomes uncomfortably apparent at times in the speechifying of some of the characters. On the other hand, as has been demonstrated, the novel exhibits a sophisticated handling of form. In addition, it possesses an attractive emotional vitality unequaled in any of the later fiction.

III   Federigo

Federigo, or, the Power of Love (1954) is an elegantly structured novel that testifies to Nemerov's belief that prose can be as fastidious a medium as verse. He felt impelled toward sophistication and elegance by his abhorrence of the slickness of much contemporary fiction: "How narrow the way, and how fastidious, even precious, must the artist be in a world so full of cheap plastic art works that every word, every feeling, every tonality, seems used up and dead and available only as its own parody."[9]

Federigo followed five years of false starts on different novels which added up to several hundred pages. Paradoxically, *Federigo* was completed in just under two months, an admirable feat in connection with a novel of so fine a grain.[10] The novel concerns the romantic adventures of Julian Ghent who, approaching middle age and sunk in boredom, writes letters to himself fictitiously signed Federigo in which he implies his wife's unfaithfulness. He leaves the letters where his wife Sylvia will inevitably come across and read them. The letters provide Julian with an excuse to be unfaithful and have the further effect of persuading his wife to be unfaithful since she has gained the reputation of infidelity in any case. Both Julian and Sylvia attract younger partners, but the affairs are impeded by the timidity of Julian on the one hand and the sexual aggressiveness of Sylvia on the other. Through a ploy by the younger partners, Julian and Sylvia find themselves reunited at the end in a manner that recalls the bedchamber scenes in some of Fielding's novels.

The device of the Federigo letter represents Julian's venturing from the monotonous safety of his middle-class existence into what he considers to be the realm of evil. The essence of his desired adultery is not that it is a concession to salacious weakness but that it signifies horror and wickedness. Julian wants the imaginative stimulus of a terrifying freedom at a time when he feels jadedly that his life is fixed within firm grooves and when he feels the ebbing of his vitality.

For much of the novel he feels that his intrigue has been a success: "he was fascinated, his entire sensibility was heightened; instead of a dull succession of moments along which he traveled like a bead on a thread, he began to see time as a house, an immense closed space of many mansions (like the Museum, in a way) with secret passages, hiding-places, alcoves, false partitions behind which whole rooms could be concealed without disturbance to the apparent dimensions as seen from outside"(p. 175)." The ending makes it evident that the freedom seized upon by Julian is illusory. Reinforcing this perception, Nemerov notes dispassionately at one point that a "man moving across an open field, under the open sky, naturally refuses to believe he is moving through a dark, narrow tunnel from which there is no escape; yet frequently, so far as his will is concerned, the latter is the more accurate version" (p. 257).

Julian's escape into evil initially involves a plunge into sensuality in the affair with Bianca. Their meeting-place, the Zoo, is almost as erotic a stimulus for Julian as Bianca herself: "Bianca would be walking, perhaps, toward the Zoo, toward the pool, where he imagined the seals, silent and unwatched now, plunging swiftly through the opacity of the water" (p. 110). Significantly, Julian feels relief that the animals, emblematic of sensuality, are caged and that their lives are carefully ordered. With characteristic caution he wants the feeling of a free fall into forbidden sexuality without upsetting his deep-seated gravitation toward order.

The relationship with Elaine Bernard is indicative of Julian's desire to mitigate not only the attrition of time, symbolized by their meeting in the Egyptian tomb, but also to recover those springs of romance which he had felt early in his marriage to Sylvia. His marriage to Sylvia had in fact been brought about by her involvement with a romantically mysterious man (who turns out to have the appropriate name of Alter) while Julian was away at war. The clandestine affair, together with Sylvia's subsequent abortion and unhappiness give her in Julian's eyes an irresistible "flavor of sad experience, of tragic possibility" (p. 26).

At its deepest level Julian's rebellion against his comfortable life with Sylvia is ultimately a revolt against the ordering of his life by the external world, time, and nature. In this sense the purpose of the fictional letters is to elicit from reality a response that will confirm his control over it: "One put to the world a hypothetical question," he reflects at one point, and "one received, it would appear, a real answer" (p. 72). Julian's pitting of the power of his consciousness against those external forces which would shape reality is derided by the apparitional Federigo in one of their occult meetings: "Hasn't it ever occurred to you," Federigo asks, "that things are profoundly and beautifully, sometimes, just what they seem to be?" (p. 220).

There are three Federigos: the epistolary Federigo invented by Julian, the literal Federigo Schwartz, a minor background character who symbolizes the independence of the external world, and the apparitional Federigo, who is a manifestation of Julian's subconscious. The emergence of this latter Federigo is an ironic and unsettling subconscious response to Julian's conscious desire to lead a double life, a development that leads to his leading his life in triplicate.

The identification of the apparition with Julian himself is made by Federigo: "To make me leave you alone," he announces to Julian, "you must be other than you are" (p. 173). Federigo appears to be clairvoyant, but is more likely the conveyor of knowledge or beliefs which lie suppressed within Julian as well as being the embodiment of some embarrassing truths about Julian—as in a hint of latent homosexuality. Sipping his drink in an "extraordinarily delicate way," Federigo is dressed "casually in slacks and a shirt open at the throat; he also wore sandals instead of shoes, and looked very much at his ease; even impudently so, thought Julian—like a proletarian poet or some such individual" (pp. 216 - 17).

In a sense Federigo is simply an extension of the fantasy/reality motif which is present in the novel, a dreamed figure who nonetheless brings to the surface the deepest currents of reality within Julian—the inside becoming the outside again. Although Federigo is not consciously summoned, Julian does intentionally fantasize a good deal. On one ironic occasion, for example, he imagines his wife being unfaithful to him by taking Hugo Alter as her lover. Since, unknown to Julian, Hugo had in fact been Sylvia's lover, the scene drolly captures Nemerov's satiric appreciation of the fluid relationship between dream and reality.

The mixing of fantasy and reality follows inevitably from Julian's ingrained skepticism about the real world. He has a "dreamlike sense of the silliness of the world. There had been about him then, what was perfectly proper for an undergraduate, a certain want of commitment to a real world, a world really and intransigently existing, and this slight imperfection, this little hollowness where there should have been belief, still formed, negatively, a part of his character, a kind of abscess. . . . He did not quite believe in the world" (p. 71). In a similar vein Julian speculates repeatedly on the propensity of life to imitate art, an assumption that underlies his sending of the Federigo letters. His ability to fantasize does have its limits, though, limits which are imposed by his sense of reality. In the fantasy in which he has an affair with Alma Alter, he imagines the two of them dying in a murder/suicide pact. In contemplating the aftermath of this, however, he finds that he is unable to generate any intensity of feeling in the survivors, Hugo and Sylvia: "So much for doing as one pleased," he reflects sadly (p. 11).

The novel is divided into two books, each of which begins with a fictitious letter of warning and each of which ends in a blending of fantasy and reality. Book One dissolves in a dream as Sylvia becomes convinced by her psychiatrist Dr. Mirabeau as well as by her own standards of reality that she had imagined the letter. Book Two ends in a masque of mistaken identities that again undermines the distinction between dream and reality. Nevertheless, the final acts of Julian and Sylvia carry a convincing sense of reality. A child is conceived on the night on which they believe—and this turns out to be a fantasy—that each is enjoying sexual gratification with someone else. Thus, as always in Nemerov, the sands of reality and the sea of fantasy change places with one another and even the most attentive mind finds itself outmaneuvered. The complexity of the ending is enhanced by its transcendence of comedy in that Julian finally rediscovers the mystery of his wife and thereby that "essential strangeness which was the beginning of love, and which is never lost but only gets forgotten, not replaced but overlaid by a number of dangerously familiar details" (pp. 16 - 17).

The action of the novel is centered in Julian's consciousness. This impressionism is counterbalanced, here as in *The Melodramatists*, by elements of formalism, but the weight of the narration is so preponderantly in favor of the subjective that physical action of any sort has a somewhat jarring effect. This explains why the mugging of Julian by Bianca and her friends has such an extraordinary impact as the rasp of her voice cuts through the softness of Julian's reveries: "Go over him good," the girl said. "The bastard's married, too" (p. 113).

The mugging serves to remind Julian and the reader of the obstinate independence of the external world. In a similar way the perception that the external world goes its own way outside the circumference of Julian's intrigue is brought home solidly in the scene in which he recalls the sight of a window cleaner who had fallen to his death: "Women, with faces averted, went carefully around the body on clicking heels and continued on their ways. . . . Nor had he himself done anything except feel an indescribable helplessness and lonely guilt, until a policeman and a doorman came running up, and the latter covered the body with a rubber mat taken from before the entrance of a building down the street. He thought now that the policeman and the doorman had been enabled to do this thing for no better reason than that they wore uniforms" (pp. 142 - 43). Thus Julian's skepticism about the ostensible reality of things and his determination to order things for himself are intermingled with his partially acknowledged sense of helplessness in coping with the external world.

The imagery of mirrors is used by Nemerov to portray the enclosed world of the mind that Julian appears so hesitant to leave. The epigraphs chosen for *Federigo* herald this motif. The first quotation from Shakespeare shows the mind projecting itself into and combining with the outer world where "it may see itself." A second quotation from Hart Crane develops the image of a solipsistic mirroring of experience which is paralleled by outer realities that "plunge in silence by."

Self-conscious and apprehensive, Julian spends a good deal of time watching himself in various kinds of mirrors, a habit that proceeds in part from his divided self, "the one to be observed (by others) as in a mirror" and the other "who did the observing, who looked out of the deep eyes but could never, by any arrangement of mirrors, look into them" (p. 7). The affair with Elaine is pursued both under the eyes of the museum's staring portraits and under the gaze of Federigo, the mirror of Julian's subconscious self.

Julian is also a conscious observer of himself. Indeed, he derives considerable pleasure from this activity, especially under the stimulus of his illicit adventure. The effect is to create a narcissistic mirror that reflects the novel's ironic subtitle among other things. The only power of love in the novel is that of self-love, as can be perceived in the museum scene:

At certain moments he had the penetrative knowledge that he himself was doing the watching, that he stood back in a corner of the gallery, slightly shielded by statue or glass case, and saw himself over some little distance taking Elaine's arm, walking her, heard himself talking to this girl (his voice sounded very odd); at these moments he watched with cynical doubt and a sneer how their heads came close together as they looked at one or another exhibit—came together and casually, whisperingly, drew apart again without a smile, without a glance, with no acknowledgment of what they both knew. (p. 183)

While Julian obviously relishes this sort of reflexive consciousness, the effect of it is to create a completely enclosed world in which "knowledge becomes a kind of cannibalism" (p. 219). Mirror consciousness becomes in fact a terror for Julian as well as a pleasurable heightening of his experience because in reflecting himself everything becomes "fluid and unstable, there was no solidity anywhere, as in a dream the most trivial object became charged with feelings of despair and fear, while the world began to fall away as in a dream" (p. 132).

The other characters also exhibit mirror vision, thereby implying that this sort of vision is inherent in the human condition rather than peculiar to Julian. Seven years after her affair with Hugo, Sylvia sees her earlier self in a mirror whose range is unimpeded by time: "She seemed to be standing back and looking at this body receiving those caresses as though it were the body of another person, for whom she felt both pity and contempt" (p. 197). Similarly, Marius Rathlin enters the rivalry with Julian for the love of Elaine Bernard thinking to himself: "I am a suitor, I am entering the arena, this that is happening to me is love" (p. 187).

The solipsistic implications of mirror vision sometimes come home to Julian, who speculates hopefully that the sensation he has of being watched may not only reflect his own self-consciousness, but may obscurely point to the existence of other observers from a Platonic world that "exactly replicated the way in which this world ought to go, and with which this world was steadily, point for point, being compared" (p. 145). The idea is further expanded in a biblical version of the postulated cosmic observer, a "They (or He, or It)" who watched both the "fall of every sparrow" and the "progress of Julian Ghent through time," divinely aware of his "most secret feeling that he ought to have been a monk or priest" (p. 10).

Federigo is an impressive novel by any standards, offering an unflinchingly unsentimental view of some fairly sophisticated characters. Nemerov structures his narrative with a baroque circularity that gracefully matches his complex epistemological themes. The fine meshing of linear and circular development can be seen in his deft use of foreshadowing. Early in the novel Julian is captivated by the view of a woman bending before a mirror at the end of a long, gloomy corridor. Moving toward him and even before she enters the light Julian recognizes her as his wife, a foreshadowing of the novel's final unmasking. The book is not without its imperfections. The subplot, for example, which involves Julian's career in the advertising business, is crude in comparison with the main plot, and is unconvincingly related to the larger action. Nevertheless, this is a minor blemish in a work that is so intellectually satisfying in its handling of both form and theme.

IV   The Homecoming Game

Nemerov's third novel, *The Homecoming Game*, appeared in 1957. He wrote the book during one summer, the bulk of it in a month.[12] While his first two novels had earned less than a thousand dollars, *The Homecoming Game*—by being turned into a Broadway play and Hollywood film—brought in bags of money: "All one winter and spring," he has noted, "my shoulder ached from carting those checks to the bank, and for six years thereafter there came every January some six to seven thousand dollars from the movie."[13]

The novel centers on the moral dilemma of Charles Osman, a history professor at a small Eastern college. Osman, a Jew who does not look Jewish, is a widower who feels guilty about his wife's death. He fails Raymond Blent, the college's football star, on a history test and thereby imperils the annual homecoming game. A strict but fair grader, Osman is appalled by the pressure brought to bear on him to change Blent's mark. In successive waves he is assailed by student delegations, Blent's erotic girl friend, Lily Sayre, the college's president, and various potentates from the business and political worlds who are benefactors of the college. In an interview with Blent, Osman discovers that the young man deliberately failed the test in order to be disqualified from playing in the game. He had taken a bribe to throw the game and in a change of heart had decided to fail academically in order to disqualify himself.

Moved by Blent's predicament, Osman decides to take charge of the situation and to allow his student to take the test over and to play in the game. He promises to return the bribe money to its criminal sources. Complicating the situation is the fact that Blent has failed not only his history test but a test in philosophy as well. The philosophy instructor, Leon Solomon, adamantly refuses to change the mark, although a painstaking intervention by Osman almost persuades him to do so. In any case the college hierarchy overrules Solomon, and Blent is permitted to play. In spite of this the team loses, since the gamblers who had bribed Blent had also prudently bribed other players on the team. Osman ends up feeling sheepish and empty, disillusioned about his foray into the world of action.

While a reasonably intelligent man in academic matters, Osman is nevertheless something of a pedant and a snob. He carries around a green book-bag from an ivy-league university as a badge of superiority over the intellectual standards which obtain at his small college. He describes the historian as examining the "outsides of past events, with a view to discovering what their insides were" (pp. 3 - 4).[14] In a modest way the dilemma regarding Blent gives him an opportunity, he believes, to assess both the inside and outside of a situation as both impartial historian and participant. He is motivated in part by feelings of ambivalence which he has always had toward football. As an undergraduate member of his university's intelligentsia, he had remained aloof from sport. Even then, however, he had felt himself involuntarily excited by the atmosphere surrounding the Saturday game. Sundays were a melancholy aftermath, the "first major hint, perhaps, for Charles, or at any rate the first hint consciously taken, of the disastrous impermanence of all things" (p. 54).

One of Osman's most self-conscious memories is that of having stood as a boy before the mirror dressed in a football uniform with a ball under his arm. In this position he had practiced "those prancing postures and snarling expressions conventionally used in photographs and cartoons of his heroes" (p. 53). As an adult his ambivalence is amplified by occasional doubts about the social and even intellectual impact of the academic world, a world that he characterizes as striving for a "serious austerity" but that as often as not achieved "shabbiness" (p. 22). Feeling that he may after all be part of an ineffectual enterprise, he plunges eagerly into what he perceives as the invigorating world of decision and action.

As with most of Nemerov's protagonists Osman reflects the dichotomy of the subjective and external worlds. Even within the sphere of the subjective he is noticeably vulnerable. He perceives himself as moving with judiciousness, for example, when in fact he is motivated in ways which he does not fully acknowledge. He is drawn to Raymond Blent, for example, not only because of the merit of his case but because Blent is physically attractive, possessing "fineness and delicacy, though it was delicacy on the magnificent or heroic scale" (p. 76). He is also influenced by his own vanity, as Nemerov satirically points up in the scene in which a pushy student delegation presses for a change in Blent's mark: "Didn't they know, didn't they even suspect by this time, that one simply didn't talk to people as they had talked to him? That what their being in such a place as this implied was, in the first place, their will to civilization, civilization with all its admitted faults and evils, civilization at all costs? But their morals, no less than their manners, belonged in a reformatory, not in a university" (p. 17).

Characteristically, Osman thinks over his annoyed reaction to the students and decides rather hastily that if he had not been so annoyed at the students he might have taken a more conciliatory line. Striving to be fair and decisive and yet haunted by the fear that he might be mistaken, he apprehensively considers walking the "high wire of the ethical" (p. 19). Ironically, and and this reflects on his intellectual presumption, he discovers once he has been out on the high wire that the situation does not depend on him alone. He discovers that Leon Solomon must also approve a change in Blent's mark. His strenuous though dignified efforts to masterfully determine the outcome of Blent's and his own situation lead belatedly to the humbling reflection that the relationships involved are too complex to manage: "For it lay in the nature of time itself that the experimental method was impossible to be applied to human action" (p. 216). Adding to his final chagrin is the humiliating perception that somewhere amidst the "heroics, dramatics, and noble expressions of principle" he had been forced to resign over an issue which in cool retrospect seemed "small, distant, and ridiculous" (p. 219).

Nevertheless, Osman's ordeal does have a maturing effect on him. For one thing, his ambition, the flagship of his existence, recedes into a dimmer light in his scheme of things: "here perhaps, after all, was the heroism that truly existed in this vale of tears; that men unflinchingly went on facing up to the noble pretense that what they wanted was success, when in truth they wanted nothing of the sort, when every success revealed itself—at once, before the testimonial dinner was over, or the ink had dried on the parchment of the diploma—as merely another piece of nonsense gained at the awful cost of having to defend it and things like it forever and ever" (p. 192). Stung by the discovery that the gamblers had determined the outcome of things in their own effective way, Osman—feeling ironically at the end that he alone is completely outside of the situation—succumbs to his cup of Ovaltine with the "cheerfulness, courage, and constancy displayed by Socrates when they brought him the hemlock" (p. 246).

Structurally, although Osman's is the focal point of view in the novel, the exploration of that point of view is dramatized through his relationships with Lily Sayre and Leon Solomon—spokes attached to the hub as it were. Lily, the candid and bewitching daughter of Herman Sayre, one of the college's affluent benefactors, seduces Osman with her air of "natural freedom, even wildness" (p. 22). In her presence he feels the encroachment of time and eagerly reaches out to her in spite of an "element of calculation" he senses in her (p. 26). Lily has the effect of crystallizing in Osman certain "vague tendencies toward the renewed possession of life, toward the assertion of oneself in the field of reality; tendencies which, for all that they are regarded as normal, had suffered the

severe shock of defeat in Charles upon the death of his wife some
years before" (pp. 124 - 25). She entices him out of his habitual in-
trospectiveness and caution: "Darling, you must have been a rather
stolid, unimaginative child," she tells him, adding that the "whole
object of life is to make it more glorious and exciting than it is, even
if you sometimes come down with a thud in the end" (p. 150).

She appeals to Osman at his two most vulnerable points, his
reawakened desire for sexual gratification and his latent snobbery.
Combining an icy elegance with youthful sensuality, she over-
powers his fastidious imagination: "She wore a black evening gown
very severely cut and unadorned, but leaving naked her shoulders
and arms. Around her neck lay a heavy, flat chain of gold. These
contrasts particularly of texture, the flesh, the funereal cloth, the
solidity and hardness of the metal, produced an impression very
striking of aristocracy and slavery together. The expensive perfec-
tion of the object of desire provoked in the beholder, as it was
meant to do, destructive longings to seize the chain, strip off the
gown, dishevel the hair" (p. 126).

Osman's relationship with Lily is an important aspect of the
novel's structure and irony because as temptress she draws him
away from the austere conditions which befit his role as a dis-
passionate judge in the Blent affair. With her he gives himself up
willingly to feelings of "helplessness, irresponsibility, and adora-
tion" (p. 189). Flying about in the Bugatti with Lily inebriated at
the wheel, Osman lets himself go, sinking euphorically into a sen-
sual, adolescent world of feeling that is wildly incongruous with his
self-appointed role as the ethical arbiter of other people's lives.
Although calculating, Lily is attracted to Osman, and although their
future would be doubtful she offers herself to him in a moment of
tenderness. Paralyzed by so direct a proposal, Osman retreats into
his conservatism: "One did not rape, even by invitation, a drunken,
unconscious female" (p. 206). Having committed himself to the
world of action, the only world that Lily respects, Osman freezes,
partly because he would be gaining from a situation which he has
pledged himself to adjudicate but mostly because he is after all a
quiet, reflective, and reserved man.

The relationship with Leon Solomon is important because it
reaches to the roots of Osman's identity and causes him to scrutinize
his motives for any trace of impurity. Solomon is an embittered, un-
comprising Jewish leftist who had entered the slumbering academic

world from a lower-class New York City background, making enemies wherever he went. As opposed to Solomon, Osman's Jewishness blends in with his surroundings. He is a "Connecticut Jew, and not Merritt Parkway Connecticut either, but of the small town, inland variety which resembled the Connecticut Yankee at least a good deal more than it did the Jew, whether rich or poor, of New York City" (p. 66).

Assuming the harsh voice of a prophet, Solomon taunts Osman with having given up the thirst for justice that he contends is the birthright of every Jew: "You are a Christian gentleman," he sneers, "or practically a Christian gentleman, and a true member of the *maspocha* of educated men" (p. 70). When the student mob materializes outside of Solomon's house, Osman finds himself identifying with his colleague's Jewishness in an unexpected way. Waiting for Solomon to draw parallels between the student mob, the Gestapo, and the gas chamber, he nervously concedes that Solomon might after all be right but that there was in fact nothing more paralyzing than a "paranoid attitude to dangers which really exist" (p. 179).

Solomon's other chief narrative function is to test the validity of Osman's proposal to Blent and to force him to be scrupulous in examining his motives. The reason for this is that Solomon is so clearly the scapegoat in the situation that he is the one man whom Osman, with his instinct for fairness, must shield from injustice. In addition, Osman senses the moral purity of Solomon in comparison with that of the powerful individuals with whose expedient cause he has aligned himself and he prefers not to offend Solomon "precisely because he could well afford to offend him" (p. 69).

Technically, *The Homecoming Game* is a suspenseful novel which may be said to combine the dramatic confrontations of *The Melodramatists* and the polished structuring of *Federigo*. The effect is to retain the energy which had become somewhat dispersed through the loose ordering of Nemerov's first novel. The various plots and themes are skillfully interlaced. This can be seen, for example, in the clever way in which Nemerov handles the description of the game. He carefully builds the narration toward the game and then depicts the sloping aftermath without in fact describing the game itself. In this way the game figures in the novel's design like the eye of a hurricane.

The satire is handled somewhat more heavily than in *Federigo* and some of the incidents—like the visit of the student delegation to Osman's office—are implausible. There are some witty moments, however, as when Nemerov illuminates the powerlessness of the academic establishment by pointing out that any combination of the college's wealthy benefactors could, if they wanted to, buy the college and "turn it into an experimental sheep farm or a Jesuit novitiate or a country club" (p. 97). Nemerov was more attentive to the landscape and to the seasons in *The Homecoming Game* than in his other novels. The descriptions of the landscape are concise and yet evocative as is Osman's grateful absorbing of his surroundings after the student delegation had met with him: "The day had begun splendidly, as autumn days regularly did here, with a brilliant frost on the grass, an air strange and keen in the mouth as the first taste of an apple" (p. 16). The autumn landscape is developed because Nemerov wanted to relate it to the annual homecoming game, which he in turn relates to rites of combat and man's relationship with the earth.[15]

His use of myth enlarges the novel's scope. In describing the bonfire, he compares it to the rain dance, which, although it did bring the rain, brought the "tribe to the pitch of enthusiasm at which they really at any rate planted the corn" (p. 91). The bonfire even includes an appropriate sacrificial victim. Similarly, the football field is said to have a kind of "totemic or sacrificial" appearance and the ritualistic prancing of the players before the game is said to reflect some "new, delightedly innocent relation with the earth itself" just as their contrasting red and white and black and white uniforms produce an effect of "cleanliness carefully preserved for the one ceremonial destruction" (pp. 209 - 10).

In spite of the satirical corona which surrounds Nemerov's use of these myths, they do finally give a certain depth to what otherwise would be a rather banal action. Musing on the controlled violence which he sees as the essence of such spectacles as football, Osman reflects persuasively that perhaps war itself in its beginning had been no more than such a ceremony. Turning over the familiar Nemerovian theme of the intermingling of imagination and reality, Osman stares into history and wistfully ponders the significance of the homecoming game: "It might be—again the odd joke of history!—that the earliest form of war was predetermined as to its outcome, having a magical purpose and a ceremonial arrangement which, entering history as garbled traditions, were misinterpreted as both real and necessary: a nasty joke" (pp. 213 - 14).

V   The Fictive Life

Nemerov's *Journal of the Fictive Life* (1965) is a diary he kept during the month from July 10 to August 10, 1963. He begins the *Journal* under the pseudonym Felix Ledger,[16] a novelist who has not written a novel for many years and who wonders why he is unable to write. In trying to answer this question, he finds himself caught up in a general exploration of art and the creative process. Unsatisfied with the indirectness of using the persona of Felix Ledger, Nemerov unmasks and then devotes most of the book to a searching examination of his own life. He writes in a time of personal crisis. His father had recently died and he himself is about to become a father for the third time after an interval of thirteen years. Gradually the *Journal* becomes a record of his past and his dreams. The dreams in turn lead to a psychoanalytical evaluation of his published writings. The book ends with the birth of his son.

The force of the *Journal* derives from its immediacy. Nemerov's sexual estrangement from his wife during the later part of her pregnancy, his guilt about his father, his fears about incorporating personal experience into a novel, and his skepticism about the future of art are intertwined convincingly and powerfully. The rawness of the book, while formally unattractive perhaps, provides a note of authenticity that caused Nemerov to think of the *Journal* as a "third way" of writing, intermediate between fiction and fact (p. 55).[17] The need for an alternative to the traditional novel is obliquely pointed up in one of Felix Ledger's whimsical reflections: "Felix would rather not be found dead in possession of the remark, The Novel is Dead. But he knew of a good many novels that showed how rumors of that sort get started." (p. 3).

Nemerov originally entitled the book *Mosaic*, meaning thereby to suggest the collagelike, nonlinear form of the work, a form which is superbly adapted to the book's contents. The progress of the narrator through the book is essentially circular. Blocked from writing fiction, he decides instead to write autobiography only to discover that he has in fact written fiction—hence the journal's title. The purpose of the Freudian analyses is to confront the subconscious by revealing the meaning inherent in its creations. The process is inevitably slow and cumulative. For this reason the shifting about in the format of the *Journal* which goes on in the first fifty pages is, from the point of view of verisimilitude at least, an important part of the book's authority.

The narrative method is that of free association. "The first principle of this writing," Nemerov notes, "is that everything is relevant;
accidents turn up and later, under close reading, prove their right to
be here by getting themselves woven into the fabric" (p. 90). Ultimately, he believed that the setting down of random observations
and recollections would stir his conscious and subconscious in such a
way that a pattern would result. The images thrown up by the subconscious circulate through the book until one has a sense of
Nemerov's most absorbing obsessions. In this way there emerges a
series of themes and variations.

Nemerov thought of his method as magical in that it fortuitously
led to the discovery of hidden and significant relationships and in
that way resembled the process of art. For this reason he was exhilarated by the thought that he had stumbled upon a new way of
doing the novel. In this connection he wrote to a friend in 1963
about the novelty of his *Journal:* "I realize that the book is a strange
one, though to anyone who is intimate with the art of letters at present, there are the plainest signs that this is The Next Phase, and in
five years every hack in the country will be doing it instead of
novels."[18] In a later interview he observed that "if you pay close attention to your life, the number of what you would otherwise think
of as co-incidences rises remarkably, just probably because of the
transformational grammar going on inside your head, always looking for pattern when it's paying heed."[19]

The effect of Nemerov's method is a curious ambiguity in which
he feels as if he is writing not about himself, but a novel about a life
similar to his. The ultimate irony is the underlying implication that
every writer faces the same impasse in trying to write about
himself—the inevitable transformation of that which was intended
to be real into the imaginative and the fictive. Even such a fictive
life, however, has a substantial universality about it in its enactment
of man's inveterate habit of discovering only what he has first of all
imagined. It might be argued that in turning the experience in
Journal of the Fictive Life over to Freudian analysis Nemerov committed himself not to the pursuit of truth but to a cumbersome,
mechanical system. It must be remembered, though, that he
thought of Freud not simply as a scientist but as a great poet.
Moreover, he uses the methods of Freudian analysis with considerable freedom, noting throughout the book the similarity between these methods and his own accustomed ways of using his imagination in writing poems and stories. In any case, whatever the

future of Nemerov's unusual narrative method, he has written a book of considerable power whose images and anxieties cling to the mind.

CHAPTER 3

Poems of the 1940s and 1950s

I   *The Poetic Vocation*

NEMEROV has described his fiction and poetry as reflecting "opposed elements" in his character. The novels tend to exhibit a satiric art and perspective whereas the poems, largely in the lyric tradition, tend to be meditative. He has described the novel as "marriage" and the poem as "infidelity" because of the steady, long-term commitment needed to produce a novel and the "violent suddenness and intermittence" that have characterized the writing of his poems.[1] Some of the reasons for his paralysis as a novelist are disclosed in *Journal of the Fictive Life*. In retrospect, he seems to have weathered his frustration with the novel with equanimity: "I simply gave up prose fiction. After all, I published—what?—three novels and two collections of short stories, and I'd be prepared to accept the judgement of the learned that they're very good but not great."[2] More important that his problems with the novel is the way in which he increasingly thought of himself as a poet during the 1950s.

In a humorous anecdote he recalls a turning point in the way in which he looked upon himself as a writer. In a meeting at Bennington in the 1950s Stanley Edgar Hyman, the head of Nemerov's department, had set out to hire a new instructor: "We were going to hire somebody, and Stanley said, we have to hire a novelist, and a voice from the back of the room, not mine, said, but Howard's a novelist, and Stanley said, Howard's a poet. So we hired Bernard Malamud instead. You know, it's trivial little things like that that mark where you have to go. I said to myself, now you know something your best friends wouldn't tell you; in fact, they've told you."[3]

Nemerov has been attracted to the mystery that has enhanced the composition of his poems, most of which come to him not as ideas but as isolated lines of verse each with its own spell: "What I love about poetry is, you don't know what you're going to do until you do it. You don't have to plan everything the way you do when you write novels."[4] His comments about poetry frequently relate to his fundamental interest in living. "For a long time," he told an interviewer, "it has seemed to me that writing poetry is a way of being interested in something other than yourself, and that that was a happiness which we're lucky to have for a little while."[5]

II The Image and the Law

Nemerov's first volume of poetry *The Image and the Law* was published in 1947, two years after his return from the war. The collection is dense, containing a great variety of poetic forms, many of which launch some major themes—the war, the phenomenal world versus the world of the mind, the urban wasteland, the anthems of autumn, the function of art. Most of the poems are skillfully related to the title and its overshadowing theme, something of an organizational feat in a first book of poems. The *image* refers to the concrete particulars that exist outside the mind. The *law* refers to the world ordered by the mind both within individuals and within culture. This is a world of relations and fixed meanings, of essences, perceived truths and moral positions. At its bleakest the world of the law is a museum of human perceptions, a collection of intellectual effigies whose lively relevance to their times has long since passed.

The world of the image with its welter of unrelated particulars is portrayed in "The Truth of the Matter," where the facts of daily disasters are served up in the Sunday papers ("Several people starved in Bucharest"). There are no accompanying meanings, however: "On Monday the wisdom of Sunday / Drifts on the gutter tides. The pale, / The staring faces, twirl around and go down. *(CP,* 9).[6] In "The Place of Value" the concrete particulars are those of a gangland slaying. A man named MacLane has his feet set in a bucket of drying cement and is thrown off a bridge: "He screamed once, / An adequate criticism and his best / Epigram" *(CP,* 17). Characteristically, having opened his poem with an absorbing scene, Nemerov steps back to contemplate it:

> The "place of value in
> A world of fact" is to supply
> Cohesiveness, weight, stability,

> And to give reason and point
> To the particular screams
> Which otherwise merely would
> Echo between empty buildings
> Or make bubbles in the water. *(CP,* 18)

Hungry for meaning, the mind is eager to assign a value to MacLane's death, but this need for order is met by an intractable silence on the part of the external world. For this reason the poem concludes that the murder was a "private fight." It is private in the sense that the relationships and motivations of the protagonists are unknown, giving the incident a quality of brutal meaninglessness.

"The Master at a Mediterranean Port" also focuses on man's relentless striving for order. Reminiscent of Wallace Stevens's poem "The Idea of Order at Key West," "The Master at a Mediterranean Port" examines the "doubleness" of the harbor scene, a scene in which man as "geometer" has imposed an order on the sea through the arrangement of his boats and docks. Resting at anchor, the boats waver between the "shadow and the real," reflecting the perceptible movement and palpable strength of the water under them as well as the shadowy, arranging mind of the observer. Beyond the harbor, however, is a different world. There the sea roils, is "turbulent, is unreflecting, deep / And deep and deep, and boils at interruption / Of wind or keel" *(CP,* 21). The churning of the deep ocean is beyond man's comprehension, a symbol of a permanently unknowable reality.

The confined arena of the harbor, however, while it pits the "law" of the mind's interpreting and arranging against the "truth" of things, at least offers some hope of understanding: "O valuable glass, / Clear harbor, floor not altogether false" *(CP,* 21). The imagery of glass is ubiquitous in *The Image and the Law* in symbolizing the smoothing out of the phenomenal world by the ordering mind. In the case of the harbor in "The Master at a Mediterranean Port," nature appears to cooperate in allowing the mind to project itself in a limited way without being contradicted by external data. In this respect the poem exhibits a marginal optimism.

The embodiment of the mind in history is the subject of "Europe," which depicts the decline of the human spirit through the stone pageantry of the saints and beasts of medieval architecture: "Saint and demon blindly stare / From the risen

stone; / Brought to a common character / Neither can stand alone"
(CP, 3).

The poem satirizes not the original inspiration which gave rise to
the great cathedrals but rather the dullness of contemporary man in
living under the shadow of these ancient effigies instead of reshaping
his world in the light of fresh perceptions: "New eucharists we
must call down / To fill our empty rooms" *(CP*, 3).

"Lot's Wife" allegorically points up the same theme. She was
turned into a pillar of salt because she looked back—a bitter symbol
of those who ingenuously seek the meaning of the present in the
rigidities of the past:

> A hard lesson to learn,
> A swift punishment; and many
> Now seek to escape
> But look back, or to escape
> By looking back: and they
> Too become monuments. *(CP*, 41)

The city, the flower of civilization, is an iterative symbol in *The
Image and the Law* for the failure of Western culture. In "The
Situation Does Not Change" New York is visualized as a necropolis
in which "Only the dead have an enduring city, / Whose stone
saints look coldly on a cold world / With the compassion of pure
form not flesh" *(CP*, 22). The speaker looks ambivalently at the
tombstone skyscrapers of the city and finds himself caught between
the intelligible though sterile images of a rigid, inherited culture
and the confusing, mutable surface of present events. He finds himself
paralyzed in contemplating the two kinds of experience:

> O Lord, we may not pray for permanence:
> Not for death, nor for destruction of cities.
> Neither moving nor still, lost in the vast
> Desert or tundra, our Atlantic time
> Coastless and without depth or place to hide
> Lord from thy sun. Like melting wax we change,
> Waiting the last shape of death at thy hand. *(CP*, 23)

Death is inevitable, therefore, in either the world of the law with its
petrified permanence or in the world of the image with its
meaningless succession of forms.

Another poem which powerfully conveys Nemerov's pessimism concerning his relationship to cultural history is "The Frozen City," which characteristically combines the stoniness of the city with metaphors of ice and coldness in a skillful streaming of visual and tactile elements. The poem offers a surrealistic, moonlit view of Manhattan in winter and combines imagistic precision with prophetic intensity:

> Cold space parted me from
> The marvelous towers
> Towards which I strained.
> With every appearance of
> Solidity the city yet
> Possessed the radiant dead
> Purity of ice, glass, reflecting
> Clearly the multitudinous stars. *(CP, 4)*

The inhabitants of the frozen city belong to a grotesque organic world of gangrenous flesh and convulsive movements, the world of generation. They are drawn from their meaningless agony by the superior organizing force of the city's culture and law into a state of existence that offers change without relief: "Some, while / I watched, died (their heads / Rolled off, this signifying / An abdication of the will) / But the cold preserved them in / Their charnel integrity" *(CP, 6)*.

In "From a Record of Disappointment" the city is associated with the "chaste paralysis / Of decided history" *(CP, 8)*. The unfolding of current history within the city is equally affected by the settling of a morbid stiffness as is seen in "Metropolitan Sunday": "Aimless and important, the / Newspapers freeze life / To the floor, the advancing / Ice-cap of every Sunday" *(CP, 25)*. If ice symbolizes the spiritual immobility of Western culture, snow symbolizes the chaotic unintelligibility of the phenomenal world. Caught up in the iconoclastic bias of contemporary empiricism, the children in "The Triumph of Education" are systematically deprived of the solace of traditional religious and ethical beliefs ("At first it may seem odd— / There isn't any God" *[CP, 14]*). The snow imagery in the poem symbolizes the draining of vitality from culture and the snow crystals that fall together into a blankness symbolize the billions of unrelated concrete particulars that defeat the mind in its search for pattern.

An alternative to the frozen city of Western urbanization is the tropical world of primitive man, an example of which is given in "Two Poems": "In Africa, whole tribes with painted rumps / Circle their fires, beating out no code / Of civil overtures, but humping up / A savage erudition to the sun" *(CP,* 10). The choice turns out to be one of industrialized decadence versus uncivilized bestiality. Furthermore, althought Western man perceives himself as having left savagery behind, what he creates is an ugly parody of his primitive origins with the green garbage of the city supplanting the forest green of the jungle: "In precise blue air / He stands, a solitaire, and drags to begin / His broken shadow through the green debris" *(CP,* 12).

The war poems in *The Image and the Law* are surprisingly restrained, a confirmation of Nemerov's later conviction that he did not grasp the significance of the war until it was well behind him. The characteristic mood of these poems is numbness, induced in part by a delayed sense of shock but also by the din of postwar America. In the poem "For W——, Who Commanded Well," for example, the speaker tries vainly to recall and to concentrate on the heroism of the officer's life and death, but is distracted by the crassness of his society in which "money is being made, and the wheels go round, / And death is paying for itself: and so / It does not seem that anything was lost" *(CP,* 36).

The distraction caused by the noisy obliviousness of post-war America is linked with the fact that this was the same society that had expediently sent its young abroad in the name of idealism. The mood of disenchantment is particularly sharp in "Who Did Not Die in Vain." The returning soldier, having left many of his fallen comrades in distant graves, finds that politicians use the silence of the dead for their own ignoble purposes ("their puppet heads / Voided comic balloons: their speaking death / Supposed his debt, and gave him much advice"). Furthermore, the returning warrior, already filled with bitterness, finds that the experience of war, far from sustaining his idealism, has contagiously left him with a "viciousness he learned to breathe" *(CP,* 17).

With considerable skill Nemerov relates the burial of the war dead to the prevailing urban necropolis motif. In "Under the Bell Jar," for example, the graves of the dead soldiers undercut the "foundations of cities: / Powerless they gain the ascendancy. / We maintain life on old battlegrounds, / Where death fattens the seed for death" *(CP,* 20). The ironic circularity of the process whereby the war dead both physically and spiritually fuel the civilization that has used them, to justify the undertaking of more wars, is portrayed with macabre and stunning conciseness.

Increasingly the mood of *The Image and the Law* becomes not only depressing but claustrophobic. Even nature is empty and oriented toward death. In "Portrait of Three Conspirators" the world is seen to revolve tediously while the "tired despotic seasons succeed / Each other forever. They sit there forever" *(CP,* 13). The poems are generally set at night and in winter or autumn. The few summer poems contain an oppressive sultriness. A representative poem is "Observation of October" in which the speaker feels a fear of "death in the weather" *(CP,* 24).

Nemerov's claims for art and the imagination are minimal in *The Image and the Law.* In "Portrait of Three Conspirators" words—instruments of poetic art—fall "coldly on the seasons as they go / Like disappointed kings to burial" *(CP,* 14). The poet addresses himself bitterly to language in a vain attempt to make the seasons and the world itself intelligible and incandescent:

> I say to them, I must die, because the world
> Is not a stage. And you are growing old,
> You are not diamond that might scratch the glass
> Of Heaven or the mind: you are the shadows
> Of posturing desire, and you effect no change
> In the position of things as they are.
> Nothing can change them. They sit there as if
> Immortal, and mutter, like actors on a stage,
> Of art and wisdom, and a change of life. *(CP,* 14)

Language and the imagination thus bend irresistibly toward meaning and enhancement even when there is every reason to doubt the mind's ability to illuminate reality.

The eye, a recurrent metaphor in these early poems, is vulnerable in that it clings to the opaque surfaces of things like a camera. The assertive prominence of the eye is described in "The Stare of the Man from the Provinces" in which the city "coruscates with eyes / Both bold and proud, of dames and gentlemen." At night, however, the inward eye takes over, and through its bizarre vision exposes the shallowness of the diurnal eye: "At night all hooligans in lonely bed / Must suffer cry of birds they had thought dead. / And diamond beak, unfashionable nails / Tear at the eyes until in sleep sight fails" *(CP,* 12 - 13). When it does try to look beyond the surfaces of things, the eye is ironically most likely to see itself. Thus, the artist in venturing into the external world is portrayed as operating in a closed circuit, like Narcissus, who in "Glass Dialectic" is "caught in simile and drowned." The lesson of Narcissus is that "you are your metaphor" *(CP*, 30). Only through the mind can intelligibility exist and yet in its search for intelligibility the mind ends up scrutinizing itself even when it thinks it is exploring the outer world. Typically, the imagery of glass—a variation on Narcissus's reflective pool—points up the theme: "This ghost will speculate in glass, is cold, / But answers to your name when it is called" *(CP*, 30).

The epitome of the mind's separation from external reality is Platonic idealism, which is the subject of "Epitaph on a Philosopher the Reports of Whose Death Have Been Grossly Minimized." The temptation for the artist to be a Platonist is depicted in the "fictive bone," which like a "disease of light, / Sheds an old sack of shadow on the ground" *(CP*, 27). The danger of pursuing idealism in the search for meaning is that the mind in its preference for abstractions has a tendency to strip external reality, leaving it with "all its thingness gone" *(CP*, 27). Art is depicted in *The Image and the Law* as ineffectual in helping to relieve man's meaningless sense of his existence. In "Advice from the Holy Tomb," for example, the speaker, dazzled by the noonday sun, reflects:

> But glass, we are glass. Wherever we would stand
> High noon will magnify light to a fault:
> Doom will consume the land.
> And your transparent heat will call a halt
> Too late. Melting, your art cannot sublime
> Fire to gold or spice, or decent salt. *(CP*, 47)

Significantly, Nemerov rejects the confident Keatsian metaphor of marble as a symbol of art, choosing fragile glass instead.

A few of the poems are faintly positive. "Unscientific Postscript," for example, places art in an ambiguous light since, although the mind's ability to discover reality is denied, the artist is encouraged to proceed even if he feels the appearances of things to be illusive:

> It is not to believe, the love or fear
> Or their profoundest definition, death;
> But fully as orchestra to accept,
> Making an answer, even if lament,
> In measured dance, with the whole instrument. *(CP*, 48)

The artist is asked to suspend both belief and disbelief in favor of an imaginatively heightened transformation of what he sees.

Another marginally affirmative lyric is "Autumnal," which Nemerov dedicated to his wife. The poem straddles the worlds of mortality and spirit, though it is weighted toward degeneration and death:

> the falling leaves resume the earth,
> Recording time upon the sodden floor;
> All energies and foreign heats retract
> And luminous at night, in rain, the mold
> Decays. It is a timely paradox
> To be considered by who works in stone. *(CP, 34)*

Within the setting of transience and decay Nemerov anticipates the inevitable waning of his wife's beauty: "Fading the flesh delineates the bone, / Indicts your face, a precious artifact." He suddenly shifts away from the mood of desolation at the end of the poem, however, in a brief tribute to the ability of love to mitigate if not offset the erosion of time: "Love is the form of stone, statue and law / As far locked from corruption of the sun / As Buddha smiling in the seamless rock" *(CP, 35)*. The quiet joy of the speaker's feeling enhances the insight that love is not a solution to anything. It is a state of being, a competing mode of experience whose value is gratefully acknowledged even when it is not understood.

The Image and the Law is rich in its variety of poetic forms, which extend from the baroque complexity of the sestina to free verse. Even in poems that are unrhymed and informally organized, though, Nemerov paid close attention to stanzaic structure. He concedes that he was imitative: "I think I was pretty much without a self to write about, and was very derivative and imitative. Ben Jonson says that's the way to do it; I've never ceased to believe it."[7] As to specific influences his standard reply is that he has had them all: "I was influenced by just about everybody, all the fashionable things. Eliot, Auden, Yeats, Empson; and through them John Donne and the metaphysical style."[8] The metaphysical style can be seen in the poem "September Shooting" with its arresting imagery: "Now is the season for dry smell of powder, / The blue smoke inciting wood and fen / To silence after the gun's report" *(CP, 36)*. The violent image of "inciting" the woods to silence is representative of Nemerov's attraction to hyperbole in this volume.

The phrasing in *The Image and the Law* is not as pure as it might have been. There are examples of polysyllabic clutter, awkward even when intended as in the coining of "Traumatic aggrandizements" in "The Frozen City." Much of the diction is harsh and surrealistically contorted. While this is suited to Nemerov's dark themes, it is at times simply cumbersome. Nevertheless, in poems like "The Place of Value," "The Situation Does Not Change," and "Autumnal" a fresh and distinctive voice can be heard. Moreover, in the use of traditional forms Nemerov shows a bold and sophisticated mastery of the most complex challenges. Taken together with his careful structuring of some strong themes, his adroit handling of tonal ironies and his skillful interlacing of symbolic motifs, the overall impression is of a formidable first book.

III   Guide to the Ruins

Guide to the Ruins, published in 1950, contains a similar range of themes to *The Image and the Law* and also exhibits a great variety of poetic forms—including ballads, fables, sonnets and epigrams. Some of the lyrics, like "Elegy of Last Resort," show the influence of T. S. Eliot and Wallace Stevens, but toward the end of this poem Nemerov's own voice is clearly audible:

> We enter again November; cold late light
> Glazes the field. A little fever of love,
> Held in numbed hands, admires the false gods;
> While lonely on this coast the sea bids us
> Farewell, and the salt crust hardens toward winter. *(CP,* 76)

If "false gods" suggests the influence of Eliot, the firm, austere imagery of November—especially the final image of the salt crust— anticipates Nemerov's later work.

Guide to the Ruins contains a number of fine war poems. The war poems are more powerful than those in *The Image and the Law* as well as being more tightly structured, vivid, and direct. "Redeployment" is an example:

> They say the war is over. But water still
> Comes bloody from the taps, and my pet cat
> In his disorder vomits worms which crawl
> Swiftly away . . .

> I know a man
> Who keeps a pleasant souvenir, he keeps
> A soldier's dead blue eyeballs that he found
> Somewhere—hard as chalk, and blue as slate.
> He clicks them in his pocket while he talks. *(CP,* 61)

As opposed to the surrealistic pyrotechnics of *The Image and the Law,* Nemerov submits more readily to the shape of experience in *Guide to the Ruins,* thereby permitting the reader to see and hear as well as to react. "Grand Central, with Soldiers, in Early Morning" is an example:

> These secretly are going to some place,
> Packing their belted, serviceable hearts.
> It is the earnest wish of this command
> That they may go in stealth and leave no trace,
> In early morning before business starts. *(CP,* 63)

Many of the war poems have a sardonic intensity—as in "The Hero Comes Home in His Hamper, and Is Exhibited at the World's Fair." Having been mutilated by an exploding mine, the speaker has been patched together by modern medicine:

> I am without facilities for sin,
> Being a lump of undistinguished skin
> Sans this and that after the mine went off,
> Beneath my feet, with an unhealthy cough. *(CP,* 64)

In *Guide to the Ruins* Nemerov makes some effort to understand the dichotomy between the realities of war and the insulated view of it that prevails in societies that send men out to kill. In "Trial and Death, a Double Feature" he sketches the conditions under which the citizenry is isolated from reality. People are made to feel genuine emotion by the purveyors of a false reality who manipulate the contours of experience:

> the Japanese the Jew
> The housewife in Berlin, any grey face
> Caught in the sunlight of a public court.
>
> Under the automatic rifles now
> They die crowded, and a good death is one
> Well in the foreground and by the green flare

> Given a candid gloss; photographers
> May pick and choose at will, their dirty thumbs
> Rifle the white eyes of the negatives. *(CP,* 71)

Nemerov brilliantly arranges the language so that the dirty thumbs on the white eyes of the negatives suddenly generate an affective experience which is equivalent in cruelty to the tortures of war. With ironic symmetry he shows how the manipulations of the filmmakers are matched by the reciprocal appetite of audiences ("Poor Platonists") for such a restructured view of experience.

A number of the poems in *Guide to the Ruins* contain religious themes. Although a nonpracticing Jew, Nemerov has shown an interest in Christian themes. In "Virgin and Martyr," for example, he centers respectfully if detachedly on the categorical imperatives of Christian asceticism:

> In place of pain why should I see
> The sunlight on the bleeding wound?
> Or hear the wounded man's outcry
> Bless the Creation with bright sound?
> I stretch myself on joy as on the rack,
> And bear the hunch of glory on my back. *(CP,* 58)

Rather like the speaker in his poem "Nicodemus" Nemerov often places himself between Judaism and Christianity, depicting Christ, for example, as an inspired Jewish prophet. The hiatus between Judaism and Christianity surfaces from time to time, however, as in "A Song of Degrees," which is about the legendary Jew who, having mocked Christ, was popularly pictured as being forced to wander the face of the earth to the end of time. Nemerov identifies with the stubborn resiliency of his mythic protagonist, whose life he portrays as emblematic of that of the Jewish people:

> Foot and hand hardened to horn,
> Nose but a hook of bone, and eyes
> Not liquid now but stone—I
> To myself violent, fiercely exult
> In Zion everywhere. *(CP,* 54)

"Sonnet" is the most poignant and searching of the religious poems. The speaker contemplates the bloody figure of Christ carved upon a crucifix. Moved by the sight of this central symbol of

Christianity, he suddenly wonders about a Christian nation like
Germany which could compassionately contemplate the cross and
yet unleash a savagery against the Jews that "bled the babies
white." The poem attains a surprising equilibrium, however, in its
conclusion: "The point of faith is that you sweat it out" (*CP*, 73).
The thrust of the conclusion lies in its universality. The enigma of
God's purpose and man's schizoid behavior is shared by both Jews
and Christians.

Although the poems in *Guide to the Ruins* are of uneven quality,
a few—like "The Lives of Gulls and Children"—are first rate. The
poem anticipates Nemerov's mature style, being set in blank verse
and containing some of his favorite figures—sea birds, children, the
epiphany of death. Children come across dead seagulls on the
beach, the "whole delicate skeletons with the hard / Hornlike feet
peacefully displayed." Watching a few loud flies feed on the
carcass, they become aware of an odor, a "sick and wrong / Smell
mingled with the heat of the salt wind" (*CP*, 79). Later they encounter a large dying gull, which stares at them out of a "steady
and majestic eye / Like a sun part baffled in cloud, / So rheumed
over with the morning of death" (*CP*, 79). The children reach out
sympathetically to the gull, which, sullen and "weakly fierce, with
hooked beak and a claw," strikes them. Chastened by their experience, the children turn for home "Bearing the lonely pride of those
who die, / And paced by the sweet shrieking of the quick" (*CP*, 80).
The poem is deeply moving without showing a hint of sentimentality. Furthermore, the impeccable mingling of narrative and lyric
elements combined with the firmness in structure and phrasing
make it one of Nemerov's finest poems.

Most of the poems in *Guide to the Ruins* are free from the
awkwardness in diction and surrealistic looseness that weakened
some of the poems in *The Image and the Law*. On the other hand,
the poems in Nemerov's second volume are less of a piece
thematically than the lyrics in his first volume. There is a pronounced sharpness and dryness in the tone of both volumes, but *Guide to
the Ruins* seems on the whole to convey a voice that is quiet, reflective, and haunted by the sense of beauty and loss. Nemerov's
success can be judged by the fact that one of the poems, "Succession," is remarkably evocative in spite of the fact that it is a fable.
The poem allegorically depicts history as a rented room whose
previous occupant, a priest, has departed mysteriously. The speaker
imagines the priest living in the room—"His naked feet in-

congrously white." The poem's genius is that it suspends itself ambiguously between allegory and dream, both delicately interfused
like the room itself—"The furnished room, the garment without
seam" *(CP,* 67). The allusion to Christ's robe gives a final heightening not only to the spectral image of the priest but to the emotion of
the poem as a whole. While not all of the poems reach this standard,
those that do point firmly in the direction of a ripening talent that
will soon come to recognize where its strength lies.

IV   The Salt Garden

Nemerov's next three volumes of poetry, *The Salt Garden* (1955),
Mirrors and Windows (1958), and the *New & Selected Poems*
(1960), are major works not only in terms of his own output but in
the wider context of contemporary American poetry. All were
produced during his years at Bennington, including the summers
spent along the Massachusetts shoreline. All reflect the happiness of
the man during that period as well as his grateful discovery of
nature.

The Salt Garden represents a conspicuous shift in mood and
themes. The preoccupations of the first two books—war, the city,
and the dissociation of the mind from external reality—are replaced
by nature and the readiness of the mind and the external world to
communicate with each other. Nemerov approached nature in these
years in a new spirit of attentiveness as his friend Reed Whittemore
has recalled: "if visited in Vermont he could be found out on long
walks naming things. Before the switch he could, to be sure, have
been found out on the same walks, but not for the same reason: instead of naming and characterizing the birds about him he would
endow them with the trappings of paradox and analogy. After the
switch he continued to be interested in paradox and analogy, but he
was more grateful for the birds he started with than he had been."[9]

The title poem "The Salt Garden" sets the tone for the collection.
The poem contains two important motifs in dialectical relationship
with each other, the wild ocean and the garden. The dialectical
method was to become as deeply entrenched a part of Nemerov's
poetic strategy as his use of analogies and his reflexiveness. The
opening alludes to man's triumph over nature, his winning of the
garden from a "difficult, shallow soil/ That, now inland, was once
the shore/ And once, maybe, the ocean floor" *(CP,* 112). The
careful inclusion of the history of the soil introduces a note of tran-

sience that undercuts the gardener's victory since, if the land oc-
cupied by the garden had been under the ocean once, there was
always the possiblity that it might revert to that state. Therefore,
although the speaker looks out confidently at "Turnip and bean and
violet/ In a decent order set," he becomes aware of the restless,
dreamlike movement of the ocean's "wrinkled green" over the sand
and of the precariousness of his garden: "And I despise what I had
planned,/ Every work of the hand,/ For what can man keep?" (*CP*,
112).

At dawn the speaker is suddenly confronted by the commanding
appearance of a large seagull on his lawn, "like a high priest/ Bird-
masked, mantled in grey." Developing the note of the bird's majesty, the speaker compares it to a merchant prince who, having
come to "some poor province," discerns nothing of value. The image of the bird and the sea coalesce to paint a painful lesson, the
teaching of the "tenant" gardener, "Green fellow of this paradise,/
Where his salt dream lies" (*CP*, 114). Images of sleep and dream
pervade the poem. They are symbols of the endless shifting of the
surface of reality and of man's vain tendency to try to arrest this
process in order to assert his dominance. The gull, emissary from
the outer world of nature, enforces the lesson of humility through
its inhuman grace and unyielding bearing. Nemerov was fascinated
by the dramatic potential of life on the border between discrete
worlds, the space between sea and garden, mind and nature, ocean
and shore, summer and winter.

Another poem which dialectically considers the relationship between man and nature is "I Only Am Escaped Alone to Tell Thee,"
an allusion to Melville's *Moby Dick*. The speaker contemplates the
portrait of a Victorian gentlewoman, stiffly prim with the assistance
of whalebone corsets. The woman's clothing and toilet symbolize
the rigidity of the human order, although there are violent,
repressive undercurrents in the language: "And maybe only
marriage could/ Derange that queenly scaffolding" (*CP*, 116). As
opposed to the word *disarrange*, which might have been chosen, the
word *derange* is ominous in its suggestion of mental instability. The
repressed energy in this outwardly tranquil woman becomes
ironically linked with the violence of whaling through the description of the corsets:

> But all that whalebone came from whales.
> And all the whales lived in the sea,

> In calm beneath the troubled glass,
> Until the needle drew their blood.
>
> I see her standing in the hall,
> Where the mirror's lashed to blood and foam,
> And the black flukes of agony
> Beat at the air till the light blows out. (*CP*, 117)

As a consumer of the whale's bones the woman is as morally responsible for the agony of the whale as the whalers. The connection is
confirmed in the ambiguous image of the needle, which is both a
stitching instrument, suitable to a lady's boudoir, and a harpoon.

A number of poems in *The Salt Garden* reflect nature as brutal
and alien even if hauntingly attractive. Seagulls are a recurring
symbol of the otherness of nature. In "The Gulls," for example, the
speaker reflects ambivalently on the "senseless beauty" of the
birds—"sweet are their bitter cries,/ As their fierce eyes are sweet;
in their mere greed/ Is grace, as they fall splendidly to feed" (*CP*,
115). At times, as in "The Goose Fish," one is left without even a
view of the gracefulness of nature even if the speaker's fascination
remains. The monstrous looking goose fish, a type of angler fish with
a primitive, shovellike jaw and serrated teeth, presents itself to the
startled lovers on the beach like a visitor from the void. The moonlit
passion of the lovers had insulated them temporarily from the outside world until they came across the "hugely grinning head" of the
dead fish. Because of the indelible nature of the experience the fish
becomes a permanent part of their love, a "patriarch" whose somber joke can neither be explained nor forgotten (*CP*, 117 - 18).

"The Winter Lightning" contains its dialectical symbols in its title. The yoking of light and snow was not the result of a search for a
metaphysical conceit, but was based upon a real if unusual experience Nemerov had had. The central symbols are flanked by another
antithetical pair, the stone and the tree, the stone a symbol of im-
penetrable rigidity while the tree symbolizes the branching out of
relationships. The forked lightning with its bony brilliance is
analogous to the tree's branches and in spite of its terrifying energy
becomes a paradigm of the poet's art:

> So may the poem dispart
> The mirror from the light
> Where none can see a seam;
> The poet, from his wintry heart

> And in the lightning second's sight,
> Illuminate this dream
> With a cold art. (*CP*, 93)

While nature is unpredictable and violent, as can be seen in the flood which destroys the bridge in "Sunday at the End of Summer," it also refreshes the mind by bringing it into touch with the world of concrete objects and sensation. Many of the poems show the ravishing of the eye by seasonal splendor—as in "The First Leaf":

> Here is one leaf already gone from green
> To edged red and gold, a Byzantine
> Illumination of the summer's page
> Of common text, and capital presage
> For chapters yet to fall. (*CP*, 96)

In other poems about nature Nemerov foregoes metaphor in order to yield to the physical details of the landscape allowing its incandescent beauty to emerge directly. "Midsummer's Day" is an example:

> A misty heat, now that the spring has gone,
> Glitters out on this hillside and the meadow,
> Over the bend where the slow river turns
> To be lost among willows. Hardly a shadow
> But the high sun seems to see through, who burns
> As from within, till the green world goes brown
> Under the skin, and the heights of summer lie
> Parched with life at the lid of the mind's eye. (*CP*, 94 - 95)

Only at the end of the passage is there a slight departure from the details of the scene. The attentiveness to natural detail reflected Nemerov's new disposition toward the importance of literal meanings. He felt that the surface of the poem should be as lucid as one could make it whereas what it means on a deeper level might be "mysterious beyond belief, because the universe is mysterious and vast, and doesn't need to mean one thing." Before being asked to venture into such depths, however, the reader should get a "more or less literal vision of what's being talked about."[10]

In poems like "A Harvest Home" and "Dandelions" one feels the poet's bliss and exuberance. The whimsical solemnity of "Dandelions" is seen in the description of the flower in seed, "those ruined spinsters, / All down the field their ghostly hair, / Dry sinners waiting in the valley / For the last word and the next life" (*CP*, 94). The poem ends with a play on words as the flowers are offered liberation from the "lion's mouth," a loose translation of "dents de lion," the French name of the flower.

The harmony between man and nature is portrayed in "Fall Song." The poem moves through the cycle of the seasons showing the responses of lovers to the seasons. In winter the lovers stand out against the white background and turn inward for warmth, away from the stinging snow. In spring the lovers are impelled to passion as everything is called to life and they find themselves blending with their surroundings: "Chameleonlike against the thing / That sets them on" (*CP*, 91). In summer they so identify with the season as to be "unseen" while in the autumn they are exposed where the "leaves grow lean / And fall." The fluctuation of seasonal energy in the lovers is affirmed as is the minor resistance which they put up. The larger perspective, though, is of broad natural changes that envelop man and sweep him toward the beauty and death that are the inheritance of all living things.

The most important change in Nemerov's portrayal of nature in *The Salt Garden* is his perception of it as emblematic. In "The Sanctuary," for example, a trout stream becomes an emblem of the mind:

> With a delicate bend and reflex
> Of their tails the trout slowly glide
> From the shadowy side into the light, so clear,
> And back again into the shadows; slow
> And so definite, like thoughts emerging
> Into a clear place in the mind, then going back,
> Exchanging shape for shade. Now and again
> One fish slides into the center of the pool
> And hangs between the surface and the slate
> For several minutes without moving, like
> A silence in a dream. (*CP*, 114)

The poem is a splendid example of Nemerov's strategy of beginning with a detailed depiction of literal reality and then reaching out through carefully considered analogies to more mysterious areas of meaning. Nevertheless, the poem dialectically registers an underlying skepticism toward this very process as can be seen in the fact that the stream finally ceases to be a "mirror" of the mind when the trout breaks the surface for a fly. At this point the speaker finds the world "again in focus," and the trout, a "shadow dammed in artifice, / Swims to the furthest shadows out of sight / Though not, in time's ruining stream, out of mind" (*CP*, 115). The poem is poised between the mind's contented weaving of relationships in its pursuit of meaning and the judicious placing of limits on this pursuit. The curvature of the poem's design places the two ostensibly contradictory elements into a circumference where each qualifies but does not annihilate the other.

If man benefits from nature's emblematic suggestiveness in certain circumstances, there are areas where the mind cannot travel. In "Deep Woods," for example, the eye attempts to follow the traceries of vines, but is defeated by the complexity of the configurations, finally turning back upon itself. The forest resists the mind's attempt to perceive it emblematically. Instead of the "tragic" crash of a dead giant oak there is the mundane weaving of more vines and branches. The scene is so untouched that it eludes the pathfinding of the mind:

> Even the Fall of Man
> Is waiting, here, for someone to grow apples;
> And the snake, speckled as sunlight on the rock
> In the deep woods, still sleeps with a whole head
> And has not begun to grow a manly smile. (*CP*, 137)

In "Zalmoxis" Nemerov combines his interests in nature and myth. The title (alternately spelled Salmoxis) refers to a cult among the ancient Thracians that ritually sacrificed bear cubs to the spirit of the mountains and forests in order to guarantee an abundance of animals for food and clothing.[11] Although the poem is about spring and about the awakening in man generated by the season, the ending focuses on the primitive vigor of nature which human wisdom must accept. As the scholar in the poem is stirred by the spring's warmth, he throws open his window and stares down the field to the "wild" hill where "on this day the sullen and powerful bear, / Drunken with deathlessness, lurches from sleep" (*CP*, 93). The mythic underpinning of the poem mingles the histories of man and animal in such a way that the antithesis between the scholar and the bear is undermined with ironic depth.

One of the most successful of the poems devoted to nature is "The Pond"—about a pond near the speaker's house that took its name from the child who drowned in it one winter. The poem is given mythic dimensions through the death of the child, Christopher, as Nemerov has explained in the *Journal of the Fictive Life*: "I drowned a child named the Christ Bearer, whose name was given the pond, and whose death is thus heroic (a hero - one who dies for his people) so that he becomes the eponymous ancestor of all that multitudinous life and death."[12] The phrase "multitudinous life and death" refers to the jungle of microscopic, ravenous creatures that are suspended in the pond. The dragonfly is an example:

> There came a dragonfly and settled down
> On a stem before my eyes, and made me think
> How in nature too there is a history,
> And that this winged animal of light,
> Before it could delight the eye, had been
> In a small way a dragon of the deep,
> A killer and meat-eater on the floor
> Beneath the April surface of the pond. (*CP*, 102)

The ascent of the dragonfly from its savage larval form to its airy mature state becomes an emblem of the themes of death and renewal that are at the center of the poem and that are given further impetus by the vanishing of the pond at the end of a dry summer. Nemerov's including in the pond's natural history the human death that has occurred there binds together human memory, art, and nature. Richly picturesque with its litany of plants and animals, "The Pond" is an evocative blending of narrative and lyric elements.

In exploring the perimeter between man and nature Nemerov presents a number of variations. The child's vision, for example, represented in "The Snow Globe," "Sleeping Beauty," "The Quarry," and "An Old Picture," provides a bond between human experience and the rest of nature. In "Central Park" the cries and light movements of the children are associated with birds:

> The broad field darkens, but, still moving round
> So that they seem to hover off the ground,
> Children are following a shadowy ball;
> Shrill, as of birds, their high voices sound. (*CP*, 130)

The reciprocal responsiveness of man and nature reflects itself in an optimistic view of the role of art. This can be seen in "The Book of

Kells," which is about the famous eighth-century illuminated
manuscript of the Gospels. Pictures of flowers, serpents, and birds
are interwined with the letters of the sacred text in a symbolic
reconciliation of nature and language. The "living word" of the
Book of Kells mysteriously carries the onlooker across time to an intense vision of the world as seen by medieval man (*CP*, 132). The
effect is to make both word and image effective mediators between
the mind and the external world. "The Book of Kells" is one of
Nemerov's most exquisite and confident poems about art.

The sequence "The Scales of the Eyes" is the most ambitious
work in *The Salt Garden*. In some ways it is a transitional work,
reflecting both the surrealistic convolutions of Nemerov's early style
and the concreteness and simplicity that are present in most of the
poems in *The Salt Garden*. The complexity of the poem was confirmed in the erudite commentary by Kenneth Burke that was attached to the first printing of the poem.[13] In part "The Scales of the
Eyes" is about nature within man, particularly about that which lies
below the surface of consciousness. This accounts for the dream
shape of much of the material and for the insistent Freudian imagery. Structurally the poem depicts an inward journey from
despair to affirmation. This inward journey is paralleled by an outward journey from winter to spring. The idiom used in making all of
the journeys in the poem is that of the stream-of-consciousness.

Although some commentators have criticized the looseness of the
sequence, Nemerov thought of it as embodying a theme and variations format "where each step has its own completion yet remains a
stage on some larger way."[14] The central theme is that of vision—as
the title implies. In the Acts of the Apostles (9:18) Paul is blinded
by God in order to stun him into being receptive to an inner vision.
When he experiences this vision, the scales of blindness slip away
from his eyes. The elaboration of the central theme somewhat
epically gathers up most of the other themes explored in *The Salt
Garden*—human versus natural order, the search for intelligibility,
the symbols of the eye and the sea.

The sequence contains eighteen numbered poems preceded by
an opening text:

> To fleece the Fleece from golden sheep,
> Or prey, or get—is it not lewd
> That we be eaten by our food
> And slept by sleepers in our sleep? (*CP*, 103)

The density and obscurity of this text is a prelude to what is to come. In order to understand it, one has to realize that it is not a message but a vision, not easily reducible to statement.

The allusion to Jason and the search for the golden fleece launches the theme of the journey. The recondite image of being "eaten by our food" refers both to the cycle of mortality that governs all life—which includes human corpses literally feeding the plants—and the voracious eating of the world by the mind, which is subsequently defeated by the inscrutable independence of the external world. The last line of the text amplifies this theme by questioning the reliability of what we take to be reality. Reality is thus visualized as a lifelong dream or trance in which the mind floats until its release by death. In connection with these themes Nemerov has written: "Our relation to experience is dominantly genitive: *my* sickness, *my* enemy, *my* death. We possess everything that possesses us."[15] In a gloomier mood he told an interviewer in the 1960s that the intellect that "questions absolutely everything, as Shakespeare shows in his tragedies all the time, destroys whatever it touches" and finally "eats up itself."[16] The mind of man, then, far from being aloof from the physical world, is here linked with the predatory cycle that underlies the rest of nature.

The second poem introduces a prominent symbol—the "zero," the still point of Nemerov's turning world—against the background motifs of sleep, blindness and darkness. The speaker falls into both death ("the wages of what you are") and sleep ("your long dream") (*CP*, 103). Although even a dreamt life might appear to be preferable to an otherwise mindless trudging toward death, the dream—a metaphor for the mind's perception of the world—is described ominously as a "monstrous bulb." The motif of the journey is contained in the "line" which is stretched out on the "liquid of the brain" while that of the seed, another important metaphor, is present in the "spore / Beyond the fires of Orion's hair." Each represents an aspect of Nemerov's irreducible pattern of reality, the curve and the line. Pursued together they bring man as close to truth as Nemerov feels he is ever likely to come.

In sections two to four the mind travels out to nature and the city as well as moving introspectively in search of itself. In the third poem the city is pictured as a tunneled necropolis with its "salt vines" of dead men's blood. The arteries of salty blood link man and nature, although the relationship has no meaning at this point. Technology dominates with its sterile lines and curves. Beyond the

city, however, nature "pounds a free way through," an exultant if
somewhat intimidating contrast to an atrophied Western culture
(*CP*, 104).

The atmosphere of darkness and fear that overshadows the
speaker's journey is strongly felt in the fourth poem:

> Beneath my foot the secret beast
> Whispers, and its stone sinews
> Tremble with strength. In the dark earth
> Iron winds its tangled nerves,
> And the worm eats of the rock
> There by the old waters.
> Down in dark the rich comb
> Gathers wrath out of the light,
> The dead ploughed down in their graves
> Record the canceled seed its doom. (*CP*, 104)

The primitivism and introspective quailing show the influence of
the poetry of Theodore Roethke on Nemerov's work at this time.
The speaker is uncertain who or where he is as he wonders where
nature leaves off and he begins. The seed reappears, but not as a
symbol of hope. The overall effect is one of unrelieved pessimism
and aimlessness.

The threat, which is metaphorically introduced in the form of the
"secret beast," becomes crystallized as the "white lion among
waters"—the city. Again, however, there is a contrast with the
equanimity of unconscious nature as the "bees hum / The honeyed
doom of time and time / Again, and riddle this underground / How
sweetness comes from the great strength" (*CP*, 104). The allusion is
to Samson's discovery of the carcass of a lion in which there were
bees and honey (Judges 14:5 - 11). In addition to continuing the
predatory motif, the scene symbolizes both death and renewal. At
this point, however, the renewal of life is simply an aspect of its un-
breakable cycle, and thus—although there is a lifting of the mood at
the end—the underlying tensions remain unresolved.

In sections five and six the speaker's introspective journey reaches
into his past. He remembers his childlike terror at the woman on a
can of Old Dutch cleanser, a whimsical image on one level but one
that is more seriously associated with maternal chastisement and
with a vague sense of sexual guilt as the word "violate" implies.
The guilt no longer remains, but the memory of it continues to disturb the speaker subconsciously: "Her anger leaves me without

stain / And white grits in the tub" (*CP*, 105). The experience thus
leaves an emotional residue ("white grits"), which rankles as much
as the original sexual impulse with its attendant guilt. In this section, as in section four, the idiom is that of the infantile voice: "I
frighten of her still" (*CP*, 105).

Section six is symmetrically related to section five in that the
speaker is overborne by an omnipotent father or god figure: "The
angry voice has sought me out / . . . What use to hide?" (*CP*,
105). The final stanza dissociates creation from the traditional
religious idea of man's stewardship: "This world is not my oyster."
Moreover, the world is not a transparent signature of God and
reality since no "slow socratic pearl grows here." The oyster image
absorbs the ubiquitous motif of the eye in the final lines: "But the
blind valves are closing / On only one grain of sand" (*CP*, 105).
The image concisely recalls the pervasive eating motif and unites it
ironically with the allusion to Blake's opening lines in "Auguries of
Innocence" about seeing the world in a grain of sand. The scales
still cover the speaker's eyes and there is an unsettling feeling in
these sections that this may be endemic to human perception.

In section seven the speaker shifts his attention from himself—
since no answers issue from the self—to the outside world. The concreteness of this external world is refreshing and reassuring in spite
of the fact that it lies hidden beneath a shroud of snow so that all
"lines were lost" (*CP*, 106). The snow clings to the blades of grass so
that it "hardly bent a blade." The effect is to suggest a successful
union of opposites in which the distinctive form of each is preserved, a hopeful analogy to the mind, which conceives of the external
world by uniting itself with it. The poem is one of the most effective
and beautiful in "The Scales of the Eyes."

From the comforting lucidity of section seven—a temporary
respite—the speaker moves to the threatening dreamscape of the
eighth poem, a reversion to the unsettled mood of the earlier sections. The air of menace arises from the image of a deserted
farmhouse, whose windows are significantly blinded by the slanting
sun. The motif of predatory eating is emphasized again as is the
feeling of faintness in falling through the darkness of the subconscious with its treacherous images of the past. Poems nine and
ten show the speaker uncertainly approaching the sea, the powerful
matrix of the natural world. The poem contains two stanzas that are
balanced antithetically, the one concerned with the "caged sea"
that moves restlessly beyond the perimeter of man's knowledge and

the other concerned with the indirectness of man's perception of the
sea:

> The spiral shell, held at the ear,
> Hums the ocean or the blood
> A distant cry, misunderstood
> Of the mind in the coiled air. (*CP*, 107)

The "coiled air" is the seashell, which in being held against the ear
echoes the sound of the ocean. The shell symbolizes both man's
dependence on an intermediary to convey the external world to him
and the probable illusory nature of that sort of derivative perception.

The background note of uncertainty heard in section nine
becomes the foreground of section ten. Having come to the sea—to
nature—for an answer to the riddle of his identity, the speaker
pauses helplessly: "Gull, where do I go now?" Though man has left
his imprint on the shore, he has left no other clue to himself.
Frustrated and disoriented, the speaker concludes that there is no
"way to go but back" (*CP*, 107). In section eleven the speaker
paradoxically enters the sea, but it is a sea of amniotic fluid. Passing
backward up the birth canal, the "tunnel with the wet wall," he
contemplates the stages of his life from the security of the womb
through the blindness, frustration and self-destructiveness of the
youthful "free" self to the philosophical pessimism of the mature
self: "Parched and shaken on a weaned world / I was in wonder
burning cold / And in darkness did rest" (*CP*, 108).

Inside the womb in section twelve the speaker listens to the
sounds of the body that surrounds him, a world that it must be
remembered is symbolically synonymous with that of the sea. The
language wavers between talk of "mother water" and a direct view
of the ocean, the matrix of nature which the mind is now willing to
enter:

> Slow cold salt, weeds washed
> Under crumbling rock ledges
> In the water cave below the root,
> Quiet the crystal in the dark,
> Let the blind way shine out. (*CP*, 108)

Immersed in the darkness of the mother ocean, the speaker

paradoxically feels on the verge of sight and longs for the scales to drop from his eyes.

Sealed off from the confusion of the culture around him ("the armies on the white roads, / The priests blessing and denouncing"), the speaker enters into a hard-won bliss in section thirteen. Tearfully he enters the "wild garden / Grown blessed" (*CP*, 109). There he feels the soothing of the "martyr's wound and the hurt heart," while the ram, a symbol of God's sparing of Isaac, stands nearby as a good omen. However, section fourteen, one of the most difficult poems in the sequence, shows the speaker regressing into an embattled state in which all past failures and disappointments flood his consciousness. Many of the major images come together in this section, adding to its density and obscurity—the eye, the salt in the blood, the vine, the shore, the pool, the cage, the beast. The poem is in fact a sort of anthology of all that has gone before and is obviously meant to symbolize not only the speaker's terror at such a visitation but his gathering of himself, including his past, for his final journey to the sea and his reconciliation with the external world.

Section fifteen focuses on an amusement park in winter, probably Coney Island:

> Cold winter, the roller coasters
> Stand in the swamps by the sea, and bend
> The lizards of their bones alone,
> August of lust and the hot dog
> Frozen in their fat. (*CP*, 110)

The ugliness of the congealed scene engenders a mood of revulsion that the poem never succeeds in throwing off. There is a minimal counterpoint, though, in the force of the sea, which "goes her own way." With his own salt blood the speaker identifies with the sea (associated with the prevailing imagery of "liquors") to announce his escape from the meretriciousness of contemporary culture: "I have sept through the wide seine" (*CP*, 110). The effect of this section is to underline the paralysis of the speaker when he addresses himself once again and finally to the question of his relationship to the culture around him. He must venture beyond the strand where man has established his culture to the naked sea and nature, the culmination of a journey that parallels the direction Nemerov himself had taken from *The Image and the Law* to *The Salt Garden*.

Sections sixteen to eighteen describe the speaker's entry into nature. Section sixteen depicts nature in varying seasons and with a purity that contrasts with the Coney Island scene:

> Snow on the beaches, briny ice,
> Grass white and cracking with the cold.
> The light is from the ocean moon
> Hanging in the dead height. (*CP*, 110)

The mood is cautious, but the language gathers itself increasingly to articulate the beauty of nature--as in the image of the gull that "rises in the snowy marsh / A shale of light flaked from a star." Moreover, beneath the crust of winter there is life both in the earth and in the roots of the speakers's psyche—"the warm dream."

Section seventeen begins in early spring when "black water breaks the ice" (*CP*, 111). The central action is of rebirth as the "horny skin is left behind." The completeness of the speaker's vision is conveyed through the persona of Teiresias, who observes a passionate mating with quiet exhilaration, a contrast to the earlier mood of sexual guilt. Vision is achieved through the renunciation of the predatory role of the mind and the glad acceptance of the mind's undemanding interfusion with nature:

> Then all was the self, but self was none;
> Knowing itself in the fiery dark
> The blind pool of the eye became
> The sailing of the moon and sun
> Through brightness melted into sky. (*CP*, 111)

The problems of philosophical dualism that had distracted the speaker have disappeared.

The final poem is a soft lyric filled with a spirit of consummation that quietly celebrates the self's discovery and bliss. Along with the scales of the eyes and the mood of disorientation the surrealistic images fall away and are replaced by fresh and limpid natural perspectives. Even mortality and mutability are gratefully accepted as the "blind worm lifts up his head / And the sparrow shakes a wet wing / In the home of little while" (*CP*, 111). "The Scales of the Eyes" is a formidable and richly complex poem both in its handling of themes and in its technical virtuosity. It lacks the strain and mannerism of the early volumes, and the surrealistic parts are superbly suited to the contents on this occasion instead of providing merely linguistic *tours de force*, as they sometimes did in the early poems. Furthermore, Nemerov's handling of prosody, especially of sound, is admirable throughout. There is the opening of section seventeen, for example: "When black water breaks the ice / the moon is milk and chalk of tooth" (*CP*, 111). The plosives in the first line ("black" and "break") skillfully register the sound of the breaking ice and flooding water.

The structure of the sequence is a thornier matter. The objection that the poem lacks firmness in direction and unity can be answered in part by a citing of its central subject—the sullen and insecure questioning by the self of its identity and of its relation to the world. Given this subject, a certain amount of drifting is both inevitable and indispensable for the sake of plausibility. At the same time, while individual poems are often carefully crafted and while the whole is unified through an effective interweaving of themes and images, the overall structure appears somewhat loose and arbitrary.

Considered as a whole, however, *The Salt Garden* has an evenness that the earlier volumes lack in addition to containing a number of first-rate poems. The poems are generally cleanly structured and they possess a convincing directness. The lines are less jagged than had been the case earlier as Nemerov begins to settle into a flexible blank verse, the frequent use of enjambment giving rise to the sort of graceful fluidity that is characteristic of his mature work. There are reminders of the earlier metaphysical style, as in "The Vacuum," but the use of this style is more polished and mellow than in the earlier work. In general the images are freshly observed and carefully particularized in accordance with Nemerov's own critical canons and the phrasing is characteristically exact and evocative. On the whole, the book is an impressive one by any standards.

V   Mirrors & Windows

Mirrors & Windows, published in 1958, represents another high point in Nemerov's career. Most of the poems sustain the happy mood which had appeared in *The Salt Garden*, the "Absent-Minded Professor" being a particularly good example:

> Now on an autumn afternoon,
> While the leaves drift past the office window,
> His bright replacement, present-minded, stays

At the desk correcting papers, nor ever grieves
For the silly scholar of the bad old days,
Who'd burn the papers and correct the leaves. (*CP*, 182)

Aware of the mind's drift toward abstractions, Nemerov again anchors his poems in the literal world—"where a teacup is more important than the universe."[17]

The title of *Mirrors & Windows* refers both to the prevailing imagery and to the dualism underlying perception. The mirrors represent the mind's reflexive recognition of itself in the objects it perceives whereas the windows symbolize both transparency and the need for an intermediary between the mind and the external world. Metaphorically, the same pane of glass serves as both mirror and window depending upon the light. The poem "The Mirror" describes the mirror world as merely analogous to the world reflected in it. It is a world that frames and thus makes comprehensible the otherwise unlimited expanse of the phenomenal world. Although the observer may be reflected in the mirror along with what he sees, there is no suggestion that mirror vision is merely solipsistic. Furthermore, as opposed to the petrified world of the photograph, the shimmering image in the mirror captures the fluidity of life so that the observer can watch the "stranger pass" (*CP*, 141).

The image of the mirror is often used to symbolize the limits of perception, though usually in a complaisant way. In "Sandpipers," for example, the speaker is struck by the courage of the migrating birds although he is unsure what this quality means to the birds themselves with their "thoughtless precisions." Nonetheless, he salutes their superior intuitiveness in "flying / From winter already, while I / Am in August." Suddenly all of the birds turn in flight and "all their bellies shine / Like mirrors flashing white with signals / I cannot read, but I wish them well" (*CP*, 153). The lines are paradoxical. The light from the birds blinds, but it also elevates the soul as in a mystical illumination.

Less optimistically, in "Maia" the mirror symbolizes solipsistic perception, although the speaker remains aware of the distinction between the mirror world and the "black water and the white / Water" which, like the world of the one and the many which they symbolize, simultaneously "race and remain" (*CP*, 194). "Endegeeste" is about an insane asylum that was once the spacious home of Descartes—an appropriate historical sequence from the speaker's point of view. Descartes, whose philosophy exalted the mirroring mind, is accepted as the shaper of modern consciousness and therefore as the maker of the wedge that divides the mind and the world. "For both of us," the speaker confesses, "the dream / Has turned like milk" (*CP*, 191). Nevertheless, the speaker remains sanely detached from the mental patients, each locked within his own Descartian tautology, and is able to maintain a cheerful skepticism, another sign of the bouyancy of *Mirrors & Windows*.

Window imagery occurs explicitly in poems like "Storm Windows," where the windows act as a stimulus to the observer's imagination as well as a filter for incoming images. Thus, "Framefull" of rain, the windows create pictorial analogies in the crushed grass beneath them like "seaweed on the tide"—an image that generates final resonances of a "lonely afternoon of memories / And missed desires" (*CP*, 144 - 45). All of the poems involve the tracing of relationships, not as part of a formal strategy, but because in Nemerov's view the perceiving of relations is implicit in any attempt to recount and explain. This is the theme of the poem "A Primer of the Daily Round." The fulcrum of the perceived relationships is analogy. The eye and mind discover analogies in the shapes of things and in the way they work. Through this process the poet gets a sense that parts of the universe belong together though he may not be able to say why or how.

A favorite emblem of Nemerov's can be seen in the poem "Trees." He sees the shape of the tree with its separate branches and single trunk as emblematic of all organic organization and as the living solution to the enigma of the one and the many. In "Shells" he sees analogies in the curvature of the sea shell that relate it to various problematic philosophical enquiries. The shell coils like "generality, from nothing to nothing." Similarly, by means of nothing but itself, it is a "stairway going nowhere, / Our precious emblem of the steep ascent" (*CP*, 145). Increasingly nature's largesse is emblematically contrasted with the sterility of culture— as can be seen in "The Statues in the Public Gardens":

> Around them rise the willow, birch, and elm,
> Sweet shaken pliancies in the weather now.
> The granite hand is steady on the helm,
> The sword, the pen, unshaken in the hand,
> The bandage and the laurel on the brow:
> The last obedience is the last command. (*CP*, 146)

"The Town Dump" employs a witty philosophical conceit to
form an analogy between the cooking compost and esoteric
knowledge—"Where Being most Becomingly ends up / Becoming
some more" (*CP*, 142). The dump becomes an emblematic window
on the relationship between man and nature, containing, as it does,
for example, the ugly products of contemporary culture: "From
cardboard tenements, / Windowed with cellophane, or simply ten-
ting / In paper bags, the angry mackerel eyes / Glare at you out of
stove-in, sunken heads / Far from the sea" (*CP*, 142). The decaying
of these objects is the first hopeful sign about them, a sign of their
return to the mainstream of nature. The refuse of man is contrasted
with the beauty of the wild birds, "Shining with light, their flight
enviably free, / Their music marvelous, though sad, and strange"
(*CP*, 144). Through its multiplicity and variety nature provides man
with paradigms of being that lead to an enrichment of perception
he would not otherwise have.

The poems in *Mirrors & Windows* are generally unsentimental in
their view of nature as can be seen in "The Loon's Cry." The
speaker stands on a bridge overlooking an estuary in one of
Nemerov's perimetric landscapes with the setting sun over the sea
on one side and the moon rising over the river on the other. The
speaker feels the balancing of the worlds on either side of him, himself as the "fulcrum of two poised immensities, / Which offered to
be weighed at either hand" (*CP*, 158). He resists a Romantic
reading of the scene describing himself as having "fallen
from / The symboled world, where I in earlier days / Found
mysteries of meaning, form, and fate / Signed on the sky" (*CP*,
159). Committed to a literal response, he is suddenly offset by the
sound of a loon's "savage" cry, which tends to confirm him in his
subdued response to nature.

Having been so reduced, however, he finds his mind released
from the staleness of conventional metaphors and unexpectedly
refreshed: "Adam I became, / Hearing the first loon cry in
paradise" (*CP*, 159). The loon seems to echo his own contempt for
man's distorting of experience through the stiff embroidery of
language—"the nouns of stone / And adjectives of glass."
Nevertheless, he becomes fraternally aware of the loon as a fellow
creature and in accepting the loon he accepts man. Within the circle of reconciliation he embraces an earlier rejected tendency to
perceive the external world as emblematic and he becomes
hospitable to the "signatures" left by living things "which leave us

not alone / Even in the thought of death, and may by arts / Contemplative be found and named again" (*CP*, 160). Therefore, at the end of the poem he allows himself to slip into metaphorical language in looking at the signal lights. The lights seem like "rubies and emeralds / Signing the cold night as I turned for home, / Hearing the train cry once more, like a loon" (*CP*, 161). He has accepted finally the naturalness of his imagination as analogous to the naturalness of the wild cry of the loon.

The desired union between man and nature is attended by lingering obscurity in spite of the consolation of isolated illuminations. This can be seen in one of the most successful poems in *Mirrors & Windows*, "A Day on the Big Branch." The poem involves a group of men, possibly college instructors, who stay up playing cards and drinking all night and then head for the woods and river in the morning "bringing only the biblical bread and cheese / and cigarettes got from a grocer's on the way, expecting to drink only the clear cold water" (*CP*, 148). In the woods nature appears to them as a home and in fact is given the features of one with "granite walls / enclosing ledges, long and flat, of limestone, / or, rolling, of lava; within the ledges / the water, fast and still, pouring its yellow light, / and green, over the tilted slabs of the floor" (*CP*, 148). The sense of ease in man's relationship with nature is supported by the run-on lines and the absence of capital letters. Suspended comfortably within the womb of nature the men unwind, sharing past experiences and settling emotionally into their wholesome surroundings.

On the way home, however, they are startled by the sight of three bridges that had been swept away by an earlier flood. The imagery becomes abruptly violent in trying to capture the sudden power of the stream, which had "twisted the girders, splintered the boards, hurled / boulder on boulder, and had broken into rubble, / smashed practically back to nature, / the massive masonry of span after span" (*CP*, 150). The mood of consolation is supplanted by the final chilling realization of the "indifferent rage" of nature. The pattern of the relationship between man and nature is typical of Nemerov. Like conjunctive planets nature and man come together for a luminous moment and then drift apart into their alien and self-absorbed existences.

A number of poems in *Mirrors & Windows* exhibit an interest in fantasy and myth. For Nemerov myth is an imaginative way of perceiving the world that lies somewhere between fact and superstition. The superstitious use of the imagination is satirized in "Lore" in which among other historical absurdities terrifying powers are attributed to women at the time of menstruation. In Nemerov's view genuine myths are both mirrors and windows reflecting both the mind of man and the variegated surfaces of the external world. "Seven Macabre Songs" uses materials from dreams, which are regarded as analogous to myth. Similarly, "Suburban Prophecy," "Moonshine," and "A Singular Metamorphosis" pursue fantasy in order to depict the strangeness in perception that occurs when the mind is released from the conventions of ordinary reality. In "A Singular Metamorphosis" a dead relation's antique escritoire, which sits sleepily in a corner of the living room, suddenly bursts into life before the startled eyes of the speaker in the poem. Significantly, no one else notices the change; it is, after all, *his* fantasy. While the others are attuned to the canned reality provided by television, the speaker finds himself more and more at a loss as the escritoire blooms profusely before his eyes: "The flowers were blue, / The fiery blue of iris, and there was / A smell of warm, wet grass." Moreover, the legs thicken and gnarl and begin to root, the "feet deep in a carpet of briony / Star-pointed with primula" (*CP*, 188).

In "Brainstorm" there is also a fantasized reversion of artifacts to their natural origins. A man alone in an upstairs room becomes aware of noises within his house and on his roof. Listening to crows walking on the roof, windows rattling and joists groaning, he becomes increasingly alarmed as the sounds press upon the membrane of his consciousness. In order to avoid the collapse of his sanity, he yields to fantasy:

> He came to feel the crows walk on his head
> As if he were the house, their crooked feet
> Scratched, through the hair, his scalp. He might be dead
> It seemed, and all the noises underneath
> Be but the cooling of the sinews, veins,
> Juices, and sodden sacks suddenly let go. (*CP*, 196 - 97)

Reaching beneath the precarious confidence of the waking self, Nemerov uncovers the subconscious torments of hybrid man, who, locked within the stronghold of consciousness, fears more than anything sinking into the ancestral and amorphous world of nature, the "green uprising and mob rule / That ran the world" (*CP*, 197). With impressive economy the poem captures the dramatic nuances of a tense psychological situation while simultaneously registering its unobtrusive statement about the place of man in nature.

The literal and the mythic are ironically juxtaposed in "Limits," which is about a group of scuba divers on a scientific exploration of the great underwater limestone caves of Florida. The language of the poem is deliberately equivocal in order to play off the empirical search of the divers or frogmen against the mythic echoes of their situation, echoes to which they are not sensitive. The speaker wonders if in a fatal crisis, the frogmen would on the verge of death abandon the rigid literalness of their vision. Pessimistically he imagines them as skeptical to the last and therefore as losing everything: "All that was lost, they fall to find, / Losing their science, which is understood" (*CP*, 198).

Figures from the Greek myths appear in "Limits" and more appear in "Cloud Seeding," the title of which recalls the bizarre sexual union of Zeus and Io. Figures from Hindu myths appear in "Maya." As he indicates in "Cloud Seeding," Nemerov employs these myths in an attempt to breach the narrow empiricism that he believes has stripped man's consciousness:

> It is my black desire to see
> The brutal and divine synod
> Gather again in thunder, ride on
> In lightning splitting the seed-pod,
> Till thought be driven as Poseidon,
> The salt-bearded teamster, drives the sea. (*CP*, 195)

The seeding of thought through myth is pursued as well in the tortuous "Orphic Scenario" and in "Mythological Beast." The beast is the unconscious, which is feared by the conscious "rider whom it will pluck down and eat" (*CP*, 181). "Orphic Scenario" involves the writing of a script for the mythic retelling of *Hamlet* on film for a contemporary audience. It is difficult and extremely allusive as can be seen, for example, in the reference to the "new Veronica"—the sultry film star Veronica Lake, who is contrasted with the penitent Veronica of the Gospels. Hamlet himself plays the role not only of tragic hero but of both redeemer and sacrificial bull in a fertility rite.

While the film makes Hamlet's ordeal intelligible, it incorporates the slickness of the contemporary media in comparison with the depth of the heroic myths. As a potential form of art, however, the film acts as all art does, arranging and amplifying human suffering and yet keeping the onlooker a tolerable distance from it so that aesthetic contemplation can take place. Nemerov calls implicitly for an art that will combine the virtuosity of recent technology with the psychic abundance of man's present and past imagination so that there will emerge the "Body of the age" (*CP*, 174). For those who mistake his stress on myth as a bit of esoteric wishful thinking, there is a somber reminder that myths mirror experience as readily as they order and heighten it: "And sometimes, in reality, / You may remember how the honey and blood / Fell from the huge lips of those murdered gods" (*CP*, 175).

A number of poems celebrate the role of art as both mirror and window in mediating between the subjective and the external world. The delicacy of the interlacing of inner and outer worlds is portrayed in "Art Song" in the evanescent metamorphosis of the seagull's feather (nature) into the artist's pen, the instrument of his imagination:

> Now the plume dowsing the poem
>   Under my hand
> Angles in waves after the lost
>   Life of the gull from land
>   Gone on horizon wings
> Where neither feather can follow nor any poet stand.(*CP*, 202)

The same motif is repeated in "Writing," where "world and spirit wed" at the "pen's point" (*CP*, 203).

The autonomy of art as a third force between mind and world is indicated in "The Map-Maker on His Art" where the cartographer expresses his creative pleasure at making the "running river a rich blue / And—let imagination rage!—wild green / The jungles with their tawny meadows and swamps / Where, till the day I die, I will not go" (*CP*, 196). While he appears to proclaim a subjective separation from the external world, his maps will necessarily reflect the outlines of that world if they are to be useful and even the colors he uses so freely mirror his contact with the various vegetative hues that exist in his own part of the world. The poem is thus an allegory of the artistic process, which involves an obliqueness in the spiraling upward from the phenomenal world to the mixed novelty and familiarity of the created form.

"Painting a Mountain Stream" explores the nature of art in a manner that anticipates Nemerov's major work "Runes" especially in its use of running water as an emblem of the reconciliation of the one and the many: "Running and standing still at once / is the whole truth. Raveled or combed, / wrinkled or clear, it gets force from losing force. Going it stays" (*CP*, 203). The role of art is thus to capture the fluidity of life and for this reason the artist is urged in looking at the stream to study "this rhythm, not this thing" (*CP*, 204). In this way the artist will capture the vitality that ripples through the living form as well as its entropic destiny, "the running down, the standing still" (*CP*, 203).

"To Lu Chi" similarly considers the theme of the mixed representational and inventive roles of art: "how to hold the axe / To make its handle" (*CP*, 199). Again, the artist is asked to consider the paradox of the one and the many in trying to capture the form of ceaselessly changing surfaces: "But look into the clear and mirroring stream / Where images remain although the water / Passes away" (*CP*, 201). The artist is told to shun the distractions of both action and speculation and to concentrate his strength on the mirroring experience:

> The waxwings, drunk on last year's rotten apples,
> Move through the branches, uttering pretty cries,
> While portly grosbeaks, because they do not drink
> That applejack, chatter with indignation. (*CP*, 201)

"Lightning Storm on Fuji" compares a nineteenth-century print of Mount Fuji by the Japanese artist Hokusai with the actual view Nemerov has of Mount Anthony looking through his Vermont window. The opening impressions stress the artificial effect of the Japanese painting, whose "gold lightning" gives "depth and huge solidity" to the scene, indicating that "this is art, not nature" (*CP*, 155). Comparing the Japanese print with the mountain before him, Nemerov finds himself wavering. While seemingly direct and authoritative, his perception of Mount Anthony is framed by the window he looks through. Moreover, his view of the mountain, seemingly a less dramatic subject than Mount Fuji, becomes less and less literal as he considers the history underlying its name. In addition he becomes influenced by the suggestiveness of the changing light on the mountain as the day wears on. Imperceptibly he finds himself in the presence of the sorts of intangible meanings that the painting had elicited: "Between eternity and time there is / Space for the terrible thought that all things fail." Unable finally to fix the relationship between art and reality, he nonetheless submits gratefully to the flow between "Mad Anthony and Hokusai and me" (*CP*, 156). The shapes, feelings, and relationships have been set down. Further definitions are not the artist's business.

Nevertheless, the final poem in *Mirrors & Windows*, "Holding the Mirror up to Nature", is a pessimistic response to the metaphysical impasse between the artist's consciousness and the external world. Based upon Dr. Johnson's strict interpretation of the representational function of art, the title contrasts ironically with Nemerov's sense of how art actually operates. Taking as his point of departure Hamlet's and Polonius's discussion of clouds and metaphor, the speaker wryly concedes the autonomy of nature beyond the reach of the artist's very limited powers: "Night clouds / go on insanely as themselves / though metaphors would be prettier" (*CP*, 207). The artist does, however, mirror that most poignant and perhaps most final of realities, his own struggle with the limitations of his art and with the inwardness of his "idiot dreams," a struggle that is inevitably carried on under the ironic shadow of death, the "buzzard" that "circles like a clock" (*CP*, 207).

The miscellaneous poems in *Mirrors & Windows* uphold the high standard of the collection. The religious poems, like "Moses" and "Ahasuerus," illustrate the often repeated comment about Nemerov that he deals with history from the point of view of the losers. One of the political poems, "The Murder of William Remington," is worth commenting on since Nemerov declared himself wary of this kind of poem because it invited the poet to focus on his own opinions, which might after all be no more valuable than anybody else's.[18] Remington, a federal civil servant, went to prison in the early 1950s, having been convicted of perjury in denying that he had fed secret information into a Soviet spy ring. While in prison he was fatally beaten with a brick by two inmates. He was reportedly murdered because of his pro-Communist sympathies. The poem captures the brutal impact of the murder as well as its social implications, but it does so obliquely within the harness of a dry, understated tone: "It is true, that even in the best-run state / Such things will happen; it is true, / What's done is done" (*CP*, 178).

Mirrors & Windows shows Nemerov to have come a very long way from the staccato style and self-conscious poetizing of the early volumes. He ran the risk of sententiousness in touching on philosophical themes, but in general he avoids pontificating by carefully building up the concreteness of his settings and the sensuousness of his language. Enhanced by a supple handling of prosody, the poems exhibit a delicate interfusion of discourse and image and of lyricism and incident, reinforced by an assured handling of structure and syntax. More than ever, beneath the broad, generous surface of the lines of blank verse, Nemerov shows his fondness for subtle changes in rhythm that ultimately have large effects on continuity and mood. The book possesses the freshness, vitality, and technical accomplishment that distinguish the creative windfall of the Bennington years.

CHAPTER 4

The Later Poems

I New & Selected Poems

*N*EW *& Selected Poems*, published in 1960, contained fifty-eight poems, of which only fifteen were new. Included among the new poems, however, was a major work—"Runes." The collection is a transitional one, a culmination of the themes and motifs of the 1950s and a prelude to the more intricate and reflexive poems of the 1960s. Nemerov described "Runes" as both a "summary of many years' partial preoccupation with its subjects and illustrations" and at the same time as the "beginning of something else."[1]

"Runes" was written in an intense two-week period—the way Nemerov likes to write. The memory of its composition has stayed in his mind as a time of "great delight" in which through the compressed time he felt himself able to write from the "midst of some sustaining center, whose variations and examinations" became the poem.[2] He has described "Runes" as a bookish poem in that it contains allusions to writers like Dante and Homer and yet he did not intend it to be esoteric. Rather, in its reflexive ruminations on the pleasures of consciousness, he meant it to sum up his principal interests as eloquently as he could and on the whole he was satisfied with what he had made of it.

The title, which derives from the enigmatic, engraved characters of the earliest German alphabet, conveys an impression of magical symbols that have been discovered and yet not adequately deciphered. "Runes" approaches phenomena in exactly this way, opening things up only to have them close in mystery again. The poem is less obsessively concerned with the dark roots of the self than was "The Scales of the Eyes" and in general possesses an orderly serenity that contrasts with the turbid restlessness of the earlier work.

104

The principal motifs are given in the opening sections—the stillness in moving things, the movement in still things, the world of generation versus that of thought and art. The principal metaphors are those of water and seed. The sequence, which is composed in blank verse, contains fifteen stanzas of fifteen lines each. The structure is polyphonic and involves complex variations on the central themes of mutability and permanence. The shape of the poem is centrifugal with the eighth stanza being dead center. Energy moves out from stanza eight in two complementary directions, the first part of the poem depicting the contraction of life from late summer to winter and the second part portraying the slow rising of new life, which finally quickens in the spring.

All of the stanzas except stanza eight are paired, the fifteenth with the first, the fourteenth with the second, and so on inward toward the center, stanza eight, the point of stasis. The pairing usually involves the use of similar or identical imagery or allusion— such as the Ulysses myth, which appears in stanzas two and fourteen. The effect of this close symmetry is the creation of a circular structure that parallels the cycling of the seasons. For Nemerov the circle is an ambiguous and necessary part of artistic structuring, representing both the "mind of God" and the "futility and unending repetition and the boredom of a bad eternity."[3] A fainter linear structure, dialectically complementing that of the circle, can be seen in the poem's arrival at spring. The strongest impression in "Runes" is that of the governing, cyclical rhythms of life, but the progress of the soul and of hope through the poem is faithful to the short term linear perspectives of human vision. To deny the impact of this vision would involve a denial, the poem implies, of human experience and therefore of the reason for poetry.

The structure of "Runes" is introduced in prelude fashion in the first rune, although the sense of contrary movement is already present in the epigraph from the *Confessions* of St. Augustine:[4]

> This is about the stillness in moving things,
> In running water, also in the sleep
> Of winter seeds, where time to come has tensed
> Itself, enciphering a script so fine
> Only the hourglass can magnify it, only
> The years unfold its sentence from the root. (*CP*, 211)

The motif of water, whether moving or still, is a recurrent one in Nemerov and is usually associated with what he called "form continuing in the changing material."[5] In addition, water imagery is usually associated with the fluidity of perception and the imagination. Still water mirrors both the external world and the completed acts of the imagination. In general the water imagery in the poem sustains the mood of reverie that is so essential to the themes connected with the passage of time. The flow of time is stilled only by death or by a fortuitous moment of illumination as the watery surface shaped by its current momentarily takes on a recognizable shape. The seed symbolizes both the inert state of death and the process of regeneration. Like the water it can represent both movement and stillness. The two motifs are brought together in the symbol of water streaming through the seed, the apex of the poem's metaphorical structuring.

Rune one is complicated by the speaker's announcement of his theme halfway through the stanza:

> That is my theme, of thought and the defeat
> Of thought before its object, where it turns
> As from a mirror, and returns to be
> The thought of something and the thought of thought,
> A trader doubly burdened, commercing
> Out of one stillness and into another. (*CP*, 212)

This theme seems initially to be unrelated to that already offered in the first part of the stanza. What happens here is that, characteristically, Nemerov pauses in the creative process to contemplate reflexively what his mind has just been doing. This gives a further dimension to "Runes" so that the pattern of movement and stillness involves not only things but also the attentive consciousness which in perception flows through things in a metamorphosis that in lucky moments generates something new and meaningful. In a letter Nemerov has written in connection with rune one: "It may have happened to you, as it so often does with me, that when you are lucky enough to be visited with a thought, the thought that follows it will not be a logical or associative consequence, but a reflexive one: Look at me, I'm thinking! So the thought about stillness in motion quite properly . . . induces the thought of thought."[6]

The "trader" metaphor at the end of the first rune becomes the dominant motif of the second rune. Nemerov's trader is Ulysses, who symbolizes movement in stillness by completing his epic journey and giving it meaning. The two arrivals attributed to Ulysses, those recorded by Homer and Tennyson, are presented as equally tenable endings. In Homer, Ulysses destroys Penelope's suitors and resumes his former life. In Tennyson, however, he "sails south / To disappear from sight behind the sun" (*CP*, 212). Tennyson portrays Ulysses as a Faustian seeker of new experience, who vanishes voluntarily into the abyss of the unknown. The two endings are crucially different in that the trader and Ulysses motifs symbolize venturing consciousness. Thus, the poem postulates very different limits for consciousness depending upon which ending is chosen. In line with the negative drifting of the first eight runes the speaker finds that he does "not know which ending is the right one."

The third rune centers on a sunflower motif and is set in late summer when eveything dies and goes to seed. While the summer scene is still replete with life, there are signs of change in the violence and desolation of the imagery and in the harrowing tone. There is a pronounced overlapping in rune two of the sunflower and trader motifs as the flowers are described as "traders rounding the horn of time / Into deep afternoons, sleepy with gain" (*CP*, 212). The imagery of gold, which unites the two motifs, is woven into a conceit that runs the length of the stanza.

In the fourth rune the gold coins issued by the sunflower—its seeds—are buried beneath the autumn soil in the "furnaces of death" (*CP*, 213). To emphasize the inertness of the seed in this section, it is alternately called a stone. The promise of movement in the stillness of the seed's apparent death lies in the genetic hieroglyphics of the future life that is contained within it—whether the seed be in the cycle of nature or in the depths of the psyche where it may one day generate "the living word." "Give us our ignorance," the speaker asks in wanting not to know the potentiality that lies within the seed—"How one shall marry while another dies" (*CP*, 213). The world outside the seed is so threatening that even embryonic life is portrayed as in peril in the image of the cock's egg *hatched* by a predatory serpent.

The fifth rune is an ironic poem to autumn. The softness of Keats's season becomes here the harsher "fat time of the year." It is also for a Jew the time of Atonement when in contrast to the harvest outside the "dry husk of an eaten heart" has nothing to offer up. Death still covers the "undecipherable seed" (*CP*, 213). The mood is bleak and the tone recriminatory and although it is autumn the atmosphere is already that of winter. Winter arrives explicitly in rune six where the stillness is paralyzing: "White water now in the

snowflake's prison" (*CP*, 214). The swirling particles of snow symbolize both chaos and a wintry view of God: "A mad king in a
skullcap thinks these thoughts / In regular hexagons." Instead of
being continuous, memory in this dead season is composed of
"atoms," which have "hooks / At either end" (past and present).
All is fragmentary, meaningless, and the direction is down: "White
water, fall and fall" (*CP*, 214). Rune seven continues the
downward movement, beginning with the biblical text "*Unstable as
water, thou shalt not excel*," Jacob's astringent prophecy for the
tribe that would descend from his firstborn son, Reuben (Genesis
49:3 - 4). The seventh rune depicts movement without stillness in
contrast to the sixth, which portrays stillness without movement. In
terms of the governing symbols of the sequence both present a form
of life that is disastrously incomplete. The unchecked and unin-
telligible movement of the seventh rune is modelled on that of contemporary technology, the bane of a "dehydrated age" whose
characteristic, ignoble activity involves "Quick-freezing dreams into
realities." This is movement without purpose and without conscience whose only constancy is to vulgarity—"till sometimes even the
Muse, / In her transparent raincoat, resembles a condom" (*CP*,
214).

Rune eight is the exact center of the sequence, the void:

> To go low, to be as nothing, to die,
> To sleep in the dark water threading through
> The fields of ice, the soapy, frothing water
> That slithers under the culvert below the road,
> Water of dirt, water of death, dark water. (*CP*, 214 - 15)

The nadir is reached when the dark, filthy water, which is usually a
crystalline symbol of hope in Nemerov's poetry, falls into the "pit
where zero's eye is closed" (*CP*, 215).

Rune nine is paired with rune seven in that both deal with the
ugliness of contemporary culture, sometimes in the same
metaphorical idiom ("this dehydrated time"). Although both poems
offer similar condemnations of the plastic age, rune nine rises
marginally at the end (as opposed to the unrelieved gloom of rune
seven) in the lyrical reference to "Mary and St. Christopher, who
both / With humble power in the world's floodwaters / Carried
their heavy Savior and their Lord" (*CP*, 215). Rune ten comple-
ments rune six in using the motif of "white water," but whereas in

six the water had been imprisoned in the snow, here it runs freely, "Rainbowed and clear and cold," and the speaker confides pleasurably that its brilliance blinds him (*CP*, 215). Similarly the inert seed of earlier stanzas "unclenches in the day's dazzle" and the renewal of life is at last promised if not as yet assured. As opposed to the chaos of rune six, the scene draws the mind to perceive relationships among the wakening creatures and to accept the water's rushing as an "utterance," which although "riddled," being a rune of nature, speaks to the reviving consciousness of the narrator (*CP*, 216, 215).

While somewhat ambivalent in its themes, rune eleven exhibits an expansion in consciousness that is equivalent to the strengthened sun and water which have melted the winter ice. In this section the speaker is able to dream, a Nemerovian metaphor for the imagination, and the dream encompasses the whole mythic cycle of Judaic / Christian history. While this history is seen to culminate in the Crucifixion, it is at least coherent, reflecting the new power of the mind to discover and create relationships. This poem thus overcomes the desolate religious imagery of its opposite number, rune five.

Rune twelve, like its counterpart rune four, focuses on the seed under the earth. Here, though, the seed bursts into life like the miraculous "stone" in *Exodus*, (17:6) and seed and water stream joyously toward their gathering shapes and destinies. The promise of the seed is foreshadowed in the image of the tree, whose leafy branches symbolize the maturation of the motif of stillness in motion as well as providing an existential answer to the paradox contained therein. Reciprocally curving toward its origins, the tree conceals its "hidden grain" under its protective bark and thus resembles the undecipherable seed from which it grew (*CP*, 216).

Rune thirteen begins with an allusion to the bloody period of imperialism portrayed in Conrad's *Heart of Darkness*, a reminder that Marlow was Nemerov's favorite fictional character as well as an echo of the trading motif of rune three.[7] The stanza suspends the joyous mood of the immediately preceding runes, rather like the contrariness of spring itself, in a review of the savagery of human history:

> To the ends of the earth
> One many-veined bloodstream swayed the hulls
> Of darkness gone, of darkness still to come,

> And sent its tendrils steeping through the roots
> Of wasted continents. (*CP*, 217)

Saline imagery mixes with that of blood and the sea recalling the salt in rune twelve and the general use of this motif in *The Salt Garden*.

The fourteenth rune is the most artfully embroidered of all of the poems in the sequence. The link with its counterpart, rune two, is made in the allusions to the lord of Ithaca and the "damask" woven by Penelope. The damask is described as "either-sided," relating it to the governing motif of this section, the meniscus, the two-sided lens of the eye. Because the meniscus is concave on one side and convex on the other, it allows the undulating waves of light to pass through as the eye focuses on some external object. The stimuli of the external world are symbolized by the water beetle, which in traveling over the meniscus "walks on drowning waters," a foreshadowing of the later dark imagery of the shroud and of death. Death is here, though, associated with "unfathomable mercies" (*CP*, 217). The ubiquitous water imagery of the sequence is included in the "raveling stream," which is associated with Penelope's tapestry and the motif of the design discovered in moving things.

The stanza is one of the most optimistic accounts of perception in Nemerov's writings. Apart from reflecting the renewed power of the speaker to draw significant relationships, the fourteenth rune depicts perception as a beautiful interchange between the mind and the external world across the fine membrane of the eye, which delicately balances the liquid sea of consciousness against the hard objects of the external world. In terms of its poise and complex interlacing of intricate metaphors, all of which interrelate effectively with the central poetic ideas of the sequence, the fourteenth rune is a stylistic *tour de force*.

The fifteenth and final rune is a blissful poem that describes the flowing of a spring stream. The scene has a sensuousness and natural vigor that contrast with the metaphysical stillness of rune one:

> To watch water, to watch running water
> Is to know a secret, seeing the twisted rope
> Of runnels on the hillside, the small freshets
> Leaping and limping down the tilted field

> In April's light, the green, grave and opaque
> Swirl in the millpond where the current slides
> To be combed and carded silver at the fall. (*CP*, 218)

The stanza contains a diaphanous purity and mood of suppleness and reconciliation that temporarily outweigh though do not overcome the darkness of death, whose voice repeatedly enters the lines. The spell works and death is held at bay as long as the "secret" is kept. The secret is associated with the soft image of "herringbones of light / Ebbing on beaches," the shifting signatures of the tide's movement. These hieroglyphic marks relate to a number of such marks in the poem, particularly those encased within the seed. The secret is identified as the self—"it is not knowing, it is not keeping, / But being the secret hidden from yourself" (*CP*, 218). Thus, the final lines symmetrically reemphasize that reflexive dimension of the sequence that had been introduced so conspicuously in rune one. The mind, though, is asked to harbor the secret without insisting on knowing it, for to do so is to invite death—not of the body since this is inevitable anyway but of the mind, which can burn itself out in turning its analytical powers relentlessly and obsessively upon itself.

"Runes" offers an absorbing exploration of the dilations of consciousness in concert with the movement and stillness of the external world. The sequence avoids the making of statements that have anything other than a structural and dramatic value as parts of the whole and it preserves throughout a sense of the hallowed mysteriousness of experience amidst the deft probing of the venturing mind, which seeks to lay open that mystery. Poetically, the sequence is filled with fine modulations in phrasing and prosody while the structure, admittedly ambitious, exhibits a sophisticated and rich network of thematic and formal crosscurrents. "Runes" reveals Nemerov at the height of his powers.

Other poems in *New & Selected Poems* are also of high quality. "Moment" is especially incisive, as can be seen in this extract:

> In the saddle of space, where argosies of dust
> Sail outward blazing, and the mind of God,
> The flash across the gap of being, thinks
> In the instant absence of forever: now. (*CP*, 211)

Nemerov's cosmic projection of the moment is marked by the complex precision that is characteristic of his later poetry. "Mrs. Mandrill" is one of the most successful of the new poems. The poem shows the tension between the proud, civilized bearing of Mrs. Mandrill and the impending humiliation of death: " 'I had not thought of this,' that lady said. / 'Involved with crowsfeet, husbands, lawsuits, I / paid it no heed' " (*CP*, 224). Detached from the consolation of religion, she describes herself as ready for her final ordeal were it not for the prospect of pain. Nonetheless, she enters nature in death and thereby undergoes an ironic "conversion" as her "wet heart spills and goes to seed" (*CP*, 225). Her conversion is paradoxical since it is associated both with the "love of God" and with the literal metamorphosis of her body into compost. The two poles of her vision are finally united in an acquiescent sense of the unity of all life, something which she had lost sight of in her matronly years. Overall, "Mrs. Mandrill" exhibits the thematic depth and technical finesse that are characteristic of the new poems in this volume.

II   The Next Room of the Dream

The Next Room of the Dream, published in 1962, contains a wealth of new poetry along with the biblical verse dramas *Endor* and *Cain.* The melancholy mood of the collection is echoed in these lines from "The Poet at Forty:" "Ah, Socrates, behold him here at last / Wingless and heavy, still enthusiast" (*CP*, 272). The "enthusiast" is present in Nemerov's thirst for knowledge, but this search is offset by an entrenched, metaphysical pessimism. The 1960s were not an especially happy period for Nemerov. There were marital difficulties in addition to other emotional setbacks, some of which are documented in the *Journal of the Fictive Life.* Many of the poems in *The Next Room of the Dream* are gloomy and anguished. The natural landscape is no longer the source of consolation it had been in preceding volumes. In "The First Point of Aries," for example, nature impassively watches man "loiter on the road to death" (*CP*, 255). The poems are usually given autumnal settings. "A Spell Before Winter," "At a Country Hotel," "Burning the Leaves," "Elegy for a Nature Poet," and "The Fall Again" are examples. The images in "The Fall Again" are uniformly somber, from the falling water that leaps in "shatterings" of light to the "drunken dark" of the heavy season in which the "rainbow shines no more" (*CP*, 262).

The joyful running water of *Mirrors & Windows* and of "Runes" has vanished. While the speaker observes nature with his usual attentiveness, it no longer speaks to him of hidden relationships and meanings. In "A Spell Before Winter" a "knowledge glimmers in the sleep of things" and the speaker announces that he can "see certain simplicities / In the darkening rust and tarnish of the time." The poem also contains the familiar, elemental motifs of water and stone, but here these motifs are submerged in the prevailing atmosphere of apprehension: "The old hills hunch before the north wind blows" (*CP*, 246).

A mood of dejection is felt as well in the antiheroic characters who are the protagonists of historical and religious poems like "Lot Later," "The View from Pisgah," and "A Predecessor of Perseus". In a discontented review of contemporary culture Nemerov portrays Santa Claus as an "overstuffed confidence man" who "teaches the innocent to want" and thus keeps the "fat world rolling" (*CP*, 238). Santa Claus is part of the statue motif in Nemerov's writings and as such he symbolizes the power of the past, of the dead.[8]

The dominant motif of *The Next Room of the Dream* is the dreamscape. The title of the book is based on an experience Nemerov had in which he interpreted one of his dreams only to discover that he was still asleep and that the interpretation was a further stage of the dream.[9] The experience is analogous to that described in "Winter Exercise" in which the speaker deliberately goes to sleep inside his dream in order to force himself to awaken. The title was drawn from the poem "To Clio, Muse of History." The poem concerns a large statue of an Etruscan warrior that was discovered to have been a forgery and was consequently moved from its place of honor in the Metropolitan Museum of Art in New York. The statue had had a powerful imaginative impact on the speaker in his youth:

> He, great male beauty
> That stood for the sexual thrust of power,
> His target eyes inviting the universal victim
> To fatal seduction, the crested and greaved
> Survivor long after shield and sword are dust,
> Has now become another lie about our life. (*CP*, 237)

Through the mysterious depth of art the warrior also taught the speaker "Unspeakable things about war that weren't in the books" (*CP*, 238).

The announcement of the forgery has the effect of invalidating both the statue's worth and part of the speaker's past. The poem thus symbolizes the arrogant destructiveness that can attend empirical knowledge, all in the "interest of truth." In becoming a nonperson, historically, the warrior enters the "next room of the dream," an ironic indication that factual history, unknown to itself, is also part of the dream of existence (*CP*, 237).

Glimpses of the dream are found in many of the poems. Goldfish, for example, cruise the "ocean of an alien dream" (*CP*, 252). In "The Fall Again" the rain spills its "dreaming strength" upon the trees (*CP*, 262). In "Winter Exercise" a man out for a walk in a blizzard enters a world of fantasy, a "walk around a dream / Whose nonsense only waking could redeem" (*CP*, 248). The distinction between the actual world and the dream world is blurred in the poem so that the speaker is unsure which world he inhabits at any one moment, especially as the scenery and characters in the two worlds are similarly familiar and improbable. The same sort of uncertainty haunts the speakers in "The View from Pisgah" and "Lot Later." The dream thus becomes the metaphor in this collection for perceived reality. It registers the mind's total response to its surroundings without the need for rational interpretation. In addition, in approaching experience in this way, Nemerov avoids becoming embroiled in epistemological discussions with himself about the validity of his perceptions. In a dream world all perceptions are equally valid.

This approach has the salutary effect on occasion of permitting Nemerov to record impressionistically the look of things with a hint of the old emblematic spirit, as can be seen in "Human Things":

> When the sun gets low, in winter,
> The lapstreaked side of a red barn
> Can put so flat a stop to its light
> You'd think everything was finished.
> Each dent, fray, scratch, or splinter,
> Any gray weathering where the paint
> Has scaled off, is a healed scar
> Grown harder with the wounds of light. (*CP*, 246 - 47)

The bittersweet evocativeness of the poem recalls Emily Dickinson.

In a number of poems Nemerov undercuts the solidity of the phenomenal world that people conventionally take for reality. The predation of the dragonfly larva, for example, an emphatically empirical phenomenon, is paradoxically described as the "small / Remorseless craving of his dream, / His cruel delight; until in May / The dream transforms him with itself" (*CP*, 255). In "Realities" a man and a woman find their behavior not only reflected in but dictated by scenarios enacted in dreams. There are occasions, however, when the vulnerability of the dream dimension is pointed up. In "De Anima" a woman stands before a window unable to see out to her lover because of the reflection of herself in the glass. She tries vainly to see beyond her own image and "half become another, / Admiring and resenting, maybe dreaming / Her lover might see her so" (*CP*, 250). The poem is an allegory of the soul's relationship with the external world: "We look to both sides of the glass at once / And see no future in it" (*CP*, 250). The importance of "De Anima" lies in its flawless poetic ambiguity and economy. The analogies between the lovers' drama and the anxieties of perception sustain the pathos of both situations. If the mind cannot know the external world, then the lovers cannot know each other. The effect of the poem is to broaden the drama of perception and to imbue it with poignancy.

In "At a Country Hotel" a widow watches her children sailing paper boats amidst the falling seeds of autumn while she dreams of her dead husband. As in "Realities" the pathos of the woman's situation is perceived by a third party, the poet, and it is he who sees the spirit of the dead husband responding to her thoughts but not getting through. He "dreams / A kindly harbor, delicate with waves, / Where the tethered dories, rocking, rise and fall, / Until the high sail heightens, coming home / To landfalls of the lily and the ash" (*CP*, 259). The only place where the living and the dead cross over is in the falling of the seeds, which signal both the "landfall" of death and the distant prospect of renewal. The poem has a tender lyricism that answers the objections of those who claim that Nemerov's poetry is overly cerebral.

The most recondite of the dream poems is "Polonius Passing through a Stage," which attempts to see Polonius through his own eyes instead of through the unsympathetic viewpoint of Hamlet. Nemerov has described the poem's subject as about a "certain kind of incoherency" in the idea of character. Polonius sinks despairingly into a dream in search of his identity, held precariously to sanity only by his platitudinous advice to Laertes: "To Thine Own Self Be True." The advice comes mockingly back to him with the implicit question: what is this self that one is to be true to? The poem ex-

plores the sources of Polonius's identity through various historical
and literary allusions, the complexity of which have been testified to
by Nemerov himself:

> there are several fathers who briefly and glancingly appear through the
> confused mutterings of the poem: There is God the Father with his "*Ten
> heavenly don'ts*," which are of course the Ten Commandments; there is
> Hamlet's father, who speakes sternly to his son about rotting at ease on
> Lethe wharf; there is King Lear, who in his madness proposes to shoe a
> troop of horses with felt in order to steal upon his sons-in-law and kill, kill,
> kill; finally, there is William Shakespeare, the father of Hamlet and so
> many others—exactly as, in a famous figure, Jehovah is the father of
> mankind generally.[10]

The parallel between Polonius and Lear as foolish old men un-
derscores the sympathetic view that is taken toward Polonius
generally in the poem. The "fathers" are of various kinds, but all
shape human identity through the transmission of culture.
Polonius's problem is that he is not clever enough to make much of
his cultural heritage: "Try to be yourself," he had been told in his
youth. "I tried. Accumulating all those years / The blue annuities
of silence some called / Wisdom" (*CP*, 252). The image is one of
the most brilliant in Nemerov's poetry, effectively dramatizing the
helpless state of Polonius, who has been shaped by others (God and
Shakespeare) whose intentions he cannot fathom. As a result he
shuffles through life on a thin program of expediency. The result is
catastrophe. He "brings the house down" (*CP*, 253) not only in
eliciting the audience's scorn but in bringing about his own death.
Moreover, his death portends the collapse that awaits the bulk of
mankind, which is equally blank about its own identity.
    Society's dream is explored in "The Daily Globe." The title in-
vites a comparison between the saga of the newspaper's collective
dream and the actual history of the globe. The paper overlooks the
natural hum of life on the globe in favor of sensationalism, concen-
trating on the "paper flowers of catastrophe" (*CP*, 242). Even those
back sections of the newspaper that purport to deal with the ordinary world, the social and obituary pages, reflect editorial distortion as the matrimonial pages contain pictures only of women and
the obituary pages show only men.[11]
    The relationship of the dream to art is outlined in a number of
poems. The alternative to an art based upon dream is realism,
which is the subject of "Vermeer." The Dutch painter is praised for

addressing himself to "What is, and seeing it as it is" (*CP*, 257). The
relationships in Vermeer's paintings are transparent and exact, part
of a "holy mathematic." Nemerov speaks of wanting to emulate the
style of this great artist and he does strive for a sort of imagistic
palpability in poems like "Goldfish," but he does not persist. His interest in consciousness is too compelling. Thus, in "Goldfish" he
slips into the ambiguities of metaphor and finally into the imaginative freedom of the dreamscape. Nevertheless, although he
sympathizes with the poet who attempts to peel the landscape back
in order to show it is a "story," he is struck in "Elegy for a Nature
Poet" by the un-storylike bluntness of the poet's death at the hands
of nature (*CP*, 261). Characteristically, he turns toward the prospect
of imaginative freedom—of the sort exemplified in "Meta-
morphoses," for example—with a sense of pleasure but also with
the mitigating sense that the artist's dreaming does not compensate
for the absence of a knowledge of the external world.

Nemerov arrives at his *ars poetica* in "Lion & Honeycomb." The
title recalls Samson's encounter with the lion's carcass in which
there was a colony of bees. The poem divides into two polarized sections. The opening lines show the speaker in a disaffected mood in
which he seems tired of virtuosity and yet is similarly bored with
those poets who stridently emphasize the "need for values" (*CP*,
277). Going his own way, he describes the role of poetry as the
recording of the "moment's inviolable presence:"

> The moment before disaster, before the storm,
> In its peculiar silence, an integer
> Fixed in the middle of the fall of things,
> Perfected and casual as to a child's eye
> Soap bubbles are, and skipping stones. (*CP*, 277)

The final images from the child's world are the honey that
mysteriously issues from the discontent of the earlier part of the
poem. The problem of dualism in perception is skirted by focusing
holistically on the experience of the present moment. The poet's
skill, honed on the villanelle and the sonnet, will be used to describe
the precise balance that the moment's particular vitality upholds
against the running down of time.

Nevertheless, the pressure of the mind to understand and the
simultaneous intuition that it never can, persist. The insatiable
hunger for meaning coexists with the awareness that the meaning

sought by the mind will inevitably turn out to be the meaning imposed by the mind. The governing motif in this perceptual drama is the eye. In "The Private Eye," for example, the eye's "lust to apprehend" is described (*CP*, 268). In "To David, about His Education" Nemerov tells his son that the world is full of "mostly invisible things" and that there "is no way but putting the mind's eye, / Or its nose, in a book, to find them out" (*CP*, 268). Similarly, in "Idea," although pure thought, a "lonely star," is associated with madness in its inviolable separation from the external world, the "independent mind thinks on, / Breathing and burning, abstract as the air" (*CP*, 248). This ingrained perversity of the mind is given pathos by the ancillary observation that all "other stars are gone" (*CP*, 249). The collapse of traditional epistemological and ethical value systems has left the mind with nowhere to turn for light but to itself in a narcissistic drama that is as poignant as it is futile.

Though the mind thirsts for knowledge, the impact of knowledge on behavior is problematic, a further refinement of the pessimistic mood that pervades *The Next Room of the Dream*. "Somewhere" is the lament of a girl who "regrets her surrender with tears." The lament is set against a background of famous women—"Yseult, Antigone, Tarquin with Lucrece, / The Brides in the Bath"—whose "careless love" led to similar misery (*CP*, 249). The implication is that the knowledge of the past offers no protection in the experience of the present. In "These Words Also" consciousness itself is seen to be the primary source of pain in contrast to the "toy kingdom" of the insects where "nobody thinks" (*CP*, 257).

The unfruitful relationship between thought and behavior is mirrored as well in *The Next Room of the Dream* in the verse drama *Endor*. The Old Testament king Saul observes wryly that those prohibitions that a man lays down for himself and others he "will do / One day, as if to spite himself" (*CP*, 278). The play involves a visit by the prophetic witch of Endor to Saul on the eve of his defeat and death. Structurally, the play is interesting because it juxtaposes an implacable determinism against man's emotional need not to know what the future holds in store. Like the other biblical play, *Cain*, which is set next to *Endor*, it lacks dramatic force. Nemerov's characteristic pursuit of fine shades tends to obviate the boldness, contrast, and intensity that are found in an effective play. Basically, both plays are deficient in action, that most indispensable ingredient of the drama.

Taken as a whole, however, *The Next Room of the Dream* is an impressive collection. It is impressive technically in exhibiting Nemerov's elegant mastery of a variety of forms, but it is also impressive in its intuitive acuteness. Karl Shapiro objected in 1967 that Nemerov's poems, while "shaped and sculptured to a turn," were somewhat lacking in sympathy and tenderness.[12] As the previous discussion has suggested, if Nemerov is absorbed by the play of consciousness, the mood of these poems is anything but cerebral. Many of the poems, such as "At a Country Hotel" and "De Anima," are deeply moving. If Nemerov's tone is fastidious and ironic, it is also compassionate. His importance as a poet derives in fact from his sophisticated application of language and rhythm to the articulation of remote and elusive emotional resonances.

III   The Blue Swallows

The Blue Swallows was published in 1967, five years after *The Next Room of the Dream,* a difficult five years, as can be seen in the *Journal of the Fictive Life.* Furthermore, Nemerov's appointments to the Library of Congress as poetry consultant and to the Department of English at Brandeis University did not provide the stimulus to his writing that Bennington had provided. In 1964 he gave some indication that he was in the process of taking stock of himself as a writer:

when the poet is older, if he has continued to write, it is at least probable that he will reach a point, either a stopping point or a turning point, at which he finds it necessary to inquire into the sense of what he has been doing, and now the question of poetic diction becomes for him extremely important, of imagination itself, of how thought ever emerged (if it did) out of a world of things.[13]

The passage indicates a pronounced tendency toward reflexiveness. For Nemerov the poetic process, especially the use of language, became a way of exploring the "question of primary perception" and of the "imagination itself." Implicit in this exploration is his belief that the answers to these large questions will be the answer to the even larger question of what makes human life distinct from that of other organisms. Looked at in this way, his poetic preoccupations seem anything but narrow.

The high quality of the poems in *The Blue Swallows* was confirmed when the book received the Theodore Roethke Memorial Award for poetry. Thematically, the poems exhibit Nemerov's

growing interest in science. Formally, the collection possesses a simplicity and abstractness that distinguish it from previous volumes.
As opposed to the preponderance of narrative and descriptive elements in many of the poems of the 1950s, a number of the poems in
The Blue Swallows come close to being statements. This is offset to
some extent by a tendency toward brevity that reflects itself in the
extensive use of short lines, sometimes involving a partial use of
rhyme.

The atmosphere is generally pessimistic, although a few of the
poems, like "Firelight in Sunlight" and "Interiors," possess a sort of
burnished warmth. In spite of the prevailing pessimism some of the
poems are flooded with light, even if it is not always a saving light.
The darkness in other poems comes largely from Nemerov's obsession with death, which is nowhere more present than in "Growing a
Ghost," a grim portrayal of his father's preparation for death.
Against this background of death is Nemerov's bleak consciousness
of the waning of his enchanted perception of nature. This can be
seen in the opening lines of "The Companions":

> There used to be gods in everything, and now they've gone.
> A small one I remember, in a green-gray stone,
> Would watch me go by with his still eyes of a toad,
> And in the branch of an elm that hung across the road
> Another was; he creaked at me on windless days. (*CP*, 355)

As the title of *The Blue Swallows* suggests, the relationship between man and nature is symbolized by birds. The relationship is
generally portrayed as alien rather than hostile. In "The Distances
They Keep," for example, the sparrows and the pheasant show "no
desire to become our friends" (*CP*, 348). The speaker speculates,
however, that this reserve in nature may ironically be its protection.
As pieces of a world "we're not responsible for," natural creatures
may through their shy separation from man "yet survive our love"
(*CP*, 349). Among other things the poem reflects Nemerov's expo-
sure to the ecological consciousness raising of the 1960s. The difference between the birds in *The Blue Swallows* and those in earlier
volumes is that, even though they occupy the symbolic space between heaven and earth, they do not have the power to evoke emblematic versions of reality for the poet-observer. Nevertheless, they
are associated with some of Nemerov's most hopeful imagery, especially that of trees. This symbolic association can be seen in
poems like "The Cherry Tree" and "Learning By Doing." In

"Learning By Doing" the presence of man is felt as menacing and this again overshadows any disappointment about nature as alien.

One of the most significant poetic statements about nature occurs in the title poem "The Blue Swallows." The poem opens with the speaker in the unusual position of looking down on some flying swallows. The darting of the swallows below reminds him of the mind's lowly location in the brain, weaving up "relation's spindrift web," just as the swallows weave designs with their flying (*CP*, 397). The speed and complexity of the birds' flight, however, prevents him from seeing what these designs are. With sympathy but also with finality he rejects the "spelling" mind's tendency to delude itself into thinking it has discovered design in nature when in fact it has imposed it. Having rejected the mind's symbolizing, he invites it to consider a new role for itself:

> O swallows, swallows, poems are not
> The point. Finding again the world,
> That is the point, where loveliness
> Adorns intelligible things
> Because the mind's eye lit the sun. (*CP*, 398)

The mind is invited to enjoy the natural forms of the external world without seeing them as coauthors of treasured moments of consciousness. The mind is then urged to glory in itself as a genuine and prolific source of responsiveness and beauty.

The only emblems left to the poet are those that portray the alien and unfathomable workings of nature. Such an emblem exists in "Between the Window and the Screen," which depicts the death of a trapped fly and the subsequent carrying off of its body by a diligent ant. "I helped not, nor oversaw the end," writes Nemerov, "Ordained to the black ant / Bearing the thin-winged heavy death" (*CP*, 386 - 87). The martial imagery of the poem connects the incident with man's bloody history, but the detachment of the insect protagonists symbolizes a savage, inhuman innocence. A similarly neutral view of nature is taken in "The Mud Turtle." Without any need for comment on Nemerov's part, the turtle generates metaphorical reverberations that expand outward from the center of the poem. The center of the poem is the moment when the turtle turns over and the speaker sees the swollen leech fastened "Softly between plastron and shell. / Nobody wants to go close enough / To burn it loose" (*CP*, 403). Left to itself, the turtle lumbers off bearing his "hard and chambered hurt / Down, down,

down, beneath the water, / Beneath the earth beneath. He takes / A secret wound out of the world."

As the incantatory, downward motion of the lines suggests, the secret lies beneath the beginnings of history and is merely recognizable though not explicable when a prehistoric creature like the dark mud turtle surfaces to remind us of what we do not otherwise remember. Like the fly and the ant, the mud turtle is an emblem of darkness, a "lordly darkness decked in filth," a "black planet," a "gloomy gemstone to the sun opposed" (*CP*, 402 - 03). The imagery magnifies the size of the turtle until it is adorned with a primeval magnificence. It emerges from its slimy womb for a transient moment as a mute and somber manifestation of the life process itself, a process that is mysteriously and pathetically flawed and yet that holds up its savage head for a moment before sinking back amorphously into its protoplasmic grave. The poem is as powerful and moving as anything Nemerov ever wrote.

In spite of the portrayal of nature as uncomfortably primitive, the mind in the later poems bends toward union with nature. In "Lobsters" the mind sinks obliviously into the "blind abyss" thinking there is "something underneath the world" (*CP*, 362). The "something" is identified as the "flame beneath the pot that boils the water." The flame symbolizes both the predatory cycle that involves both man and lobster, and includes eventually whatever fathomless force it is that drives the world. In "Landscape with Figures" the middle-aged flirtation of a man and woman is seen in retrospect as a pleasurable falling into nature, into the "green sleep of the / Landscape, the hooded hills / That dream us up & down" (*CP*, 348). The conformity between man and nature is enforced artfully through the image of the hooded hills, which rise and fall like the inflamed breasts of Mrs. Persepolis. Caught by the tide of passion, the two consider entering nature's dream if they can persuade themselves to throw down the barrier of self-consciousness.

Similarly, in "The Beekeeper Speaks and Is Silent" the beekeeper imagines himself sinking into the well of being, becoming a bee first—

> And then the single-minded hive itself,
> And after that the blossoming apple tree
> Inside the violation of the swarm—
> Until I am the brute and fruitful earth,
> Furred with the fury of the golden horde,

> And hear from far upon the field of time
> The wild relentless singing of the stars. (*CP*, 402)

The mind's submersion in nature is given impetus by Nemerov's image of man as a marooned creature. In "The Human Condition," for example, man is suspended absurdly between his mind and body. Increasingly in the poetry Nemerov wrote during the 1960s, man is depicted as a dangerous creature. The stream in "The Breaking of Rainbows," for example, struggles to throw off the foulness that man has dumped into it and for the moment succeeds—"Leaping and dancing and singing, forgiving everything"(*CP*, 400). Man's abuse of nature is echoed in his abuse of himself. In "Enthusiasm for Hats" the quiet neighborhoods of the affluent are places where "people keep / Hidden in filth a broken relative" (*CP*, 368).

Nemerov devotes a complete section of *The Blue Swallows*—"The Great Society"—to a sardonic study of the grievous effects of social and political mismanagement. In "Christmas Morning" a conventional, snow-frosted village on a greeting card is juxtaposed with the news of a Buddhist priest immolating himself in protest against American involvement in the Vietnam war. The boldness of the language in the poems about society can be felt in "Money," which scrutinizes the now defunct design of a U.S. nickel:

> one side shows a hunchbacked bison
> Bending his head and curling his tail to accommodate
> The circular nature of money. Over him arches
> UNITED STATES OF AMERICA, and, squinched in
> Between that and his rump, E PLURIBUS UNUM,
> A Roman reminiscence that appears to mean
> An indeterminately large number of things
> All of which are the same. (*CP*, 369 - 70)

The bluntness and colloquialism, which are characteristic of the later poetry, are given a sharp edge through the underlying anger. Just as the buffalo was pushed into extinction by greed, the great society is propelled narcissistically by the "circular nature" of money into a callous destructiveness that is only partially masked by a nebulous idealism.

The artists who become socially aware are no help, as can be seen in the satirical poem "A Relation of Art and Life." The socially

committed poets are depicted derisively as "savage sages" who seek
to bring catastrophe under a "copyright, and doom to its publication" (*CP*, 376). The poets are flanked by similarly ineffectual academics, "master ham and doctor clown," whose pedestrian prose
equivocates about the "Word that was no word" (*CP*, 378).

Nemerov's approach to social injustice is sometimes oblique and
muted. In "The Sweeper of Ways," for example, the sweeping of
leaves from public paths by the old Negro is both a reflection of his
servile social status and of his dignity as part of the grace of
autumn. In an article about the poem Nemerov compared the
futility of the man's sweeping to the labors of Hercules.[14] Nonetheless, the effective work of the sweeper in performing his
seemingly hopeless task moves the speaker to an admiring recognition of the man's conscious adjustment to his lot. Burdened with a
history of social inequality that he cannot avoid, the man expresses
the only pride he is permitted to reveal in a skillful performing of
his limited task. This is the meaning of the last line, which declares
that he "can do nothing, and is doing that" (*CP*, 406). The poem
succeeds by being an aesthetic study and a sensitive delineation of
human dignity rather than by means of condemnation.

In spite of the somber shading given *The Blue Swallows* by the
poems about nature and society, many of the lyrics are suffused
with light. Nemerov focused on the capacity of light to act across
distance in an invisible manner.[15] Thus, light imagery is used to
signify the mind as in "Interiors" and "Celestial Globe:" "The candle of the sun, / The candle of the mind, / Twin fires that
together / Turn all things inside out" (*CP*, 395). Ironically, however, the mind's ability to illuminate by turning things inside out is
contiguous with its mortality, as can be seen in "The Flame of a
Candle:"

> Miracle! the soul's splatter and flap
> Aloft, enlightened lamb
> That spurting through the beastly trap
> Is able to say *I am*
> *That I am*—
> Our fathers lived on these
> Desperate certainties;
> Ate manna in the desert, it is said,
> And are dead. (*CP*, 386)

The soul's triumphant freeing of itself from the body like the flame arising from the wax is polarized against the certainty of death, which ironically reunites soul and body. The light of life is thus as frail as it is hallowed. In "Small Moment," for example, it is described as a "light that shudders in the leaves" (*CP*, 407).

The intertwining of mind and sun is present throughout *The Blue Swallows*. In "Thought" the play of light through the foliage and among the "minnow waves" on the shore is likened to the mind passing across the world making its "differences / At last unselfishly / The casualties of cause" (*CP*, 393). Similarly, in "One Way" the mind, through its instrument language, is wedded to the phenomena of the external world like "sunlight / On marble, on burnished wood, / That seems to be coming from / Within the surface and / To be one substance with it" (*CP*, 395). At the end of the poem thought is described as the fire in the diamond, which itself stands small and alone against the encroaching gloom of death and meaninglessness.

Increasingly the poems picture the world in scientific terms. "The First Day" involves a witty juggling of the questing mind and the intractable external world:

> Below the ten thousand billionth of a centimeter
> Length ceases to exist. Beyond three billion light years
> The nebulae would have to exceed the speed of light
> in order to be, which is impossible: no universe.
> The long and short of it seems to be that thought
> Can make itself unthinkable. (*CP*, 345)

What makes the external world appear intelligible is the lens of the eye, which like a movie film supplies an "image, a thin but absolute membrane whose surfaces / Divide the darkness from the light while at the same time / Uniting light and darkness." The lines contain strong echoes of the creation story in Genesis. The eye's movie creates a pseudoreality that gives the illusion of progressing through real time and space. Primitive culture, which is dominated by the imaginative simplicity of religion, is symbolized by the black and white silent film. Modern culture is more subtle, and is represented by the color, sound film.

The wit of the poem lies in the playing off of scientific truths against poetically imaginative ones. The initial impression of the mind's clumsiness in arriving at an exact knowledge of the cosmos gives way to a qualified affirmation of its own powers: "For 'nothing in the universe can travel at the speed / Of light,' they say, forgetful of the shadow's speed." With its own projector, the imagination, which traditionally lives in the shadows, records its version of reality. Nemerov sets limits on the mind, however, by noting dryly that the "Fall already is recorded on the film," an ironic comment on the retarding effect of cultural tradition on the progress of knowledge.

A simpler use of science occurs in "Firelight in Sunlight." The winter scene combines brilliant exterior sunlight with the fire of apple logs inside. The scene evokes a sense of the whole cycle of nature since the logs in generating heat are merely releasing the original energy of the sun that had been transferred to them in the past. Therefore, there is what the speaker regards as a noteworthy meeting in the poem between the old sun, supposedly spent, and the new, which falls in "silvered gold / Through the fern-ice forest" on the window (*CP*, 407). The recovery of the old sun provides the speaker with hope that the mysteries of man's past and of his nature may be similarly released through the "logs" of language that have been used in constructing literary masterpieces. The meditation offers the speaker hope that his own poetic language will cross time and matter releasing its light in the minds of future generations.

"This, That & the Other" involves a debate between a scientific realist (This) and a Romantic (That). In order to break the stalemate between their respective viewpoints, each yields a bit and attempts to look out at the world from the other's point of view. Eventually each is able to correct the bias in his vision without depending on the other for help. That, for example, pulls up at one point recognizing that he is about to revert to subjectivism by straying from physics into theology. Their reconciliation is sealed in the mutual recognition that a mysterious "Other" is involved in reality in a way that makes both their viewpoints simultaneously inconclusive and promising: "The Other is deeply meddled in this world. We see no more than that the fallen light / Is wrinkled in and with the wrinkling wave" (*CP*, 360).

If Nemerov found science stimulating within its range, so too were myth and religion. In "Beyond the Pleasure Principle" man turns passionately and repeatedly toward myth in order to satisfy some long forgotten need in himself. Although mythic vision is viewed as childlike, it is also a paradigm of all knowledge. This can be seen in the seriocomic poem "Projection" in which sophisticated adults desperately try to attain the child's clarity of vision:

> To stand here, on these ladders,
> Dizzy with fear, not daring to look down,
> Glue on our fingers, in our hair and eyes,
> Piecing together the crackling, sticky sheets
> We hope may paper yet the walls of space
> With pictures any child can understand. (*CP*, 389)

Similarly, in "To a Scholar in the Stacks" a professor enters the world of myth through the ostensibly arid route of the library only to find his imagination enlivened so that the bookstacks become the labyrinth of Crete and he himself is transformed into the legendary Theseus. As the scholar slips into the desiccated rituals of his profession, he loses his earlier potent sense of imaginative contact with myth. The conclusion of the poem suggests, however, that this sense will return in periods of "darkness and deep despair." At such a time the scholar will become Theseus again and will become the "Minotaur, the Labyrinth and the thread / Yourself; even you were that ingener / That fled the maze and flew—so long ago— / Over the sunlit sea to Sicily" (*CP*, 361). The "ingener" is Daedalus, who symbolizes the artist and who is therefore the sublime apex of the scholar's metamorphosis.

Myth excites the imagination into perceiving history as a "dream within a dream" as the speaker puts it in "Departure of the Ships" (*CP*, 364). For the imagination the external world is an unfolding and yet cyclical story which speaks to the child within even the most cultivated observer. For science there is no story, only painstaking descriptions based upon minute observation of the hard shell of the external world. For the mind that has been floating in the reveries of myth and the thin air of abstractions, the sharply visualized descriptions of science are refreshingly concrete. The limitation of science as opposed to myth is that it tends to atomize knowledge as can be seen in "In the Black Museum" where it shears off the diversity of relationships between things until at last there is "only one of everything" (*CP*, 389).

In combining the data of scientific observation with his usual skeptical exploration of perception, Nemerov addresses himself in *The Blue Swallows* to issues that are at the forefront of contemporary thought. The risk with this sort of poetry is that it can become esoteric and sententious. On the whole he evades this problem by creating tensions within the poems between belief and skepticism, empiricism and Romanticism, and mind and feeling that turn the poems into absorbing dramas of the subjective life. In addition, by making the poems the subjective adventures of his observers, he hopes to generate a picture of the subjective life that can become a basis, perhaps the only basis possible, for unity between himself and the reader.

Technically, *The Blue Swallows* exhibits an ambitious range of poetic forms. In addition to the usual blank verse, for example, there are a number of short-lined poems, including both trimeter and dimeter. The rhythm of all of the poems is more subtly flexible and colloquial than ever. Nemerov shows himself as much a master of baroque art as ever, but he shows a keener interest than in earlier volumes in matching his complex forms to the exigencies of his themes. In "Sarajevo," for example, he uses the intricate form of the sestina. In this form the same last words are used in different order to end the lines in each of the six stanzas. The fastidious elegance of the form gives the poem the appearance of a minuet and this skillfully mirrors the mood of pre-1914 aristocratic Europe which is the portentous subject of the poem. The poem is one of a number of remarkable technical achievements in *The Blue Swallows*. With justified assurance Nemerov shows himself equally at home with the formalities of past poetic styles and the more relaxed prosody of the present.

IV   Gnomes & Occasions

Gnomes & Occasions, published in 1973, is a slim volume though not a meager one. At the same time, considering that six years had passed since the publication of *The Blue Swallows*, the fifty-nine short lyrics in *Gnomes & Occasions* do not strike one as prodigious. Nemerov was not troubled by personal problems in this period. Moreover, he had settled happily into the Department of English at Washington University in St. Louis. In addition his work was finally beginning to receive the sort of critical attention it deserved. He did, though, experience the sort of block that had earlier overtaken him as a writer of fiction and that he discussed in *Journal of the Fictive Life*.

The poems are varied and uneven. About half of them are epigrammatic "gnomes." Some, like "Lines & Circularities" and "The Painter Dreaming in the Scholar's House," are substantial

and among Nemerov's best works. The subjects vary a great deal—
riddles, science, art, the war in Vietnam, his sister's suicide,
autumn. The diction and syntax continue to move toward infor-
mality and simplicity and yet the verse is somewhat austere. The
mood, however, is mellow in comparison with *The Blue Swallows*
and *The Next Room of the Dream*. This is especially apparent in the
geniality of poems like "Extract from Memoirs":

> Surely one of my finest days, I'd just
> Invented the wheel, and in the afternoon
> I stuck a bit of charcoal under the bark
> And running it along a wall described
> The cycloid curve. When darkness came, I sang
> My hymn to the great original wheels of heaven,
> And sank into a sleep peopled with gods. (*CP*, 415)

The mellowness of the mood proceeds from an underlying tone of
acceptance that had replaced the pessimism of the 1960s. Also
noteworthy is the soft intermingling of scientific and religious
perspectives.

The changed mood is reflected in the relaxed approach to
spirituality in "A Memory of My Friend" and in the serene
acknowledgment of the mind's isolation from the senses and the external world in "Analogue":

> You read the clicking keys as gibberish
> Although they strike out sentences to sense.
> So in the fluttering leaves, the shoaling fish,
> The continuum nondenumerable and dense,
> Dame Kind keeps rattling off her evidence. (*CP*, 442)

The mind's isolation is balanced by the speaker's confidence that
nature is eloquently writing some sort of story and that this is im-
printed hierographically on his own senses. His connection with
nature is thus absolute even if it is incomplete.

In his fifties Nemerov felt grateful to be writing any poetry at all,
and this underlying feeling of gratitude seeps into most of the
poems in *Gnomes & Occasions*. He told an interviewer in 1973 that
the writing of poetry was a "great privilege."[16] The joy of composing comes across warmly in jeweled miniatures like "The Crossing,"
"Late Butterflies," and "Above":

> Orange translucent butterflies are cruising
> Over a smoke of gnats above the trees
> And over them the stiff-winged chimney swifts
> Scythe at the air in alternating arcs
> Among the roofs where flights of pigeons go
> (slate as the roofs above and white below) (*CP*, 443)

The collection abounds with aphorisms and riddles. The aphorisms found in poems like "Philosophy" and "The Death of God" are set against the riddles in poems like "Power to the People" and especially "Quaerendo Invenietis." Nemerov's fascination with riddles stems from his sense that they represent the "very basis of poetry."[17] What he meant is that, like memorable poetry, good riddles remain mysterious even when the answer to them is known. This can be felt in the poem "Mystery Story," where the answer to the riddle is provided at the outset. Riddles also resemble poems in that the answers precede the questions. The answer to the riddle is like the title of a poem, which often becomes meaningful (without losing its mysteriousness) only when one has worked carefully through the poem. Nemerov likes the surprise of riddles, which he sees as parallelling poetry in revitalizing experience by altering its mundane appearance.

"Quaerendo Invenietis" (Seek and ye shall find), contains three riddles. The answer to the first riddle is the alphabet ("I am the combination to a door / That fools and wise with equal ease undo"). The answer to the second is the tone arm of a record player ("It is a spiral way that trues my arc"). The answer to the third riddle is a sentence ("Without my meaning nothing, nothing means" *CP*, 413). Significantly, two of the answers have to do with language, which for Nemerov is the supreme riddle in its mysterious reconciliation of the mind and the external world. Considering the prosaic nature of the answers, the riddles in "Quaerendo Invenietis" contain oddly mystical language. Even the tone arm shares in this heightening as it is visualized moving toward "central silence." The image suggests religious depths that seem curiously out of place. They can be explained by the attitude of the observer in the poem, an attitude that can be described as a Taoist concentration on the flowering of even the most ostensibly mediocre manifestation of being. In some respects this is reminiscent of the contemplative serenity in the poems of the 1950s, but the mood is more hallowed and austere than in these earlier volumes.

In harmony with this shift in mood the poems in *Gnomes & Oc-*

casions show a relaxed acceptance of the suggestiveness the mind perceives as latent in the ordinary workings of the external world. In "Lines & Circularities," for example, the speaker listens to the music of Bach on the record player in a way that recalls the riddle in "Quaerendo Invenietis":

> I watch the circling stillness of the disc,
> The tracking inward of the tone-arm, enact
> A mystery wherein the music shares:
> How time, that comes and goes and vanishes
> Never to come again, can come again. (*CP*, 416)

The rebirth of Bach on the record involves a blending of sublimity (the music) and the mundane (the record player). For this reason the occurrence is called a "silly" miracle, which, although it will not "save" the world, is nonetheless "miraculous" (*CP*, 416 - 17).

Nemerov retained his sense of the ruined world, as can be seen in "The Puzzle," but he responds gratefully to life in these poems not only in spite of but because of its flaws. "Snowflakes" is an example:

> Not slowly wrought, nor treasured for their form
> In heaven, but by the blind self of the storm
> Spun off, each driven individual
> Perfected in the moment of his fall. (*CP*, 440)

The return to nature as emblematic is as striking as Nemerov's renewed loyalty to the only life he knows—even if that life is thought to be illusive. There is as well an attitude of undisturbed indifference to the epistemological doubts that scarred the poems of the 1960s. The doubts persist, as can be seen in "Knowledge," but they are absolved in a benedictory calm that is diffused throughout the collection. The mind's relationship with nature is informed by a feeling of comfort as in "Beginner's Guide" and "The Poet as Eagle Scout":

> I said to the stone, "Am I standing all right?"
> "How's this for running?" I said to the stream.
> "Is it bright enough for you?" I asked the light.
> And I told my dream, "You're a damn fine dream." (*CP*, 441)

The imagination's revived pleasure in its surroundings encompasses art as well. In "Breughel: The Triumph of Time" the world is depicted as a "ramshackle traveling show" that cyclically and arbitrarily "does whatever's done and then undoes it" (*CP*, 417 - 18). "The World as Breughel Imagined It" presents a similarly bizarre portrait of reality in which whatever is "proverbial becomes pictorial" (*CP*, 429). Thus, if people proverbially go "crawling up a rich man's ass, they must be seen to do so." After the proverbial lore that underlay the paintings has been forgotten by subsequent generations, Breughel becomes difficult to decipher. Nonetheless, through the durable clarity of art a modern observer can intuit the meanings so that, struck with the aptness of some of Breughel's pictorial allegories, he will take Breughel's word in "many matters wherein we have no further warrant / Than that his drawings draw enciphered thoughts from things" (*CP*, 429). The mind gravitates toward art because unlike the opaque phenomenal world it possesses a meaning whose value is axiomatic and which does not depend upon being completely understood.

"The Painter Dreaming in the Scholar's House" was written in memory of the modernist painters Paul Klee and Paul Terence Feeley and was read at the inauguration of the president of Boston College in 1968. The poem thus has the amplitude of a formal public statement. The meditation arises principally from Nemerov's reflections of Klee's paintings, but he obviously feels a strong sense of identification with Klee's breadth as both artist and scholar. Moreover, both poet and painter depend upon the mediation of language, whether language take the form of brushstroke or word. Similarly, the mind of the painter, like that of the poet, goes out into the forms of the surrounding world—into a tree, perhaps— where it become "incarnate" (*CP*, 435). At that point the painter paints the tree, which is then indistinguishable from his charged idea of it. The poem ends with the "light" of the external world going forth in search of the eye, a paradoxical reversal of the earlier part of the poem, which focused on the eye and the mind in pursuit of the external world. The eye of the artist plays so important a role that the world is vacant without it. Instinctively realizing this, as it were, the world seeks out the eye in an attempt to confirm its own being.

Nemerov continues to rely on science in *Gnomes & Occasions* to provide him with metaphor. In "Solipsism and Solecism" the light cast by the sun is seen to be solipsistic and therefore a model of the mind. The sun sees only what it illuminates and therefore unlike the

moon has no knowledge of shadow or night. Elaborating whim-
sically on the motifs of solitariness and light, the poem contains a
glaring solecism in the last line: "He'd be appalled at what he's
done" (*CP*, 414). The grammatical error echoes the note of disloca-
tion that issues from the ironical fact of the sun's blindness with
respect to the world of shadows. The awkwardness of this defect in
vision is wittily symbolized in the solecism. The notion of two-sided
realities is also found in "The Tapestry," "Hide & Seek," and
"Creation Myth on a Moebius Band." "Creation Myth on a
Moebius Band" shows Nemerov using a scientific metaphor for his
longstanding inside/outside motif, a variation of which appears in
the top/bottom motif of "Solipsism & Solecism." A. F. Moebius
(also spelled Möbius) was a nineteenth-century German mathemati-
cian who developed a mathematical demonstration to form a continuous one-sided surface in which the inside literally becomes the
outside. The Moebius strip thus resembles language in allowing the
outside world to pass to the inside and vice-versa. The poem illustrates Nemerov's sense of the continuity between being and consciousness as opposed to the biblical notion of a single act of creation by an isolated divine consciousness.

The inside/outside motif is also elaborated in "Questions" where
the "radar of the mind" receives back what it sends, "but
modified. / The breath of language goes out on the wind, / The
drumming on the eardrum comes inside" (*CP*, 442). The motif is
given ironic treatment in "Druidic Runes." The poem recounts the
history of astronomy from the simple observations of the Druids,
made with the naked eye, to the sophisticated technology of the
radio astronomers of today. In radio astronomy the mind goes forth
"without the eye" into the "realm of number pure" and significantly its purely mathematical idiom surpasses the range and precision
of the eye and the telescope. Thus, the outside can only become the
inside when the external data are of limited complexity: "It was as
if the lip / Of silence learned to intimate / In integers that it might
mate / Its dark selfhood to any mind / Consenting to go blind"
(*CP*, 419). The aesthetically satisfying vividness of the eye's pattern-
ing is offset by its simplicity, a state of affairs that Nemerov appears
finally willing to accept with equanimity.

Gnomes & Occasions contains a number of topical poems on
American society including "Power to the People," "The Poverty
Programs," and "On Getting Out of Vietnam." Nemerov's skep-
ticism about the value of such poems is balanced by his reluctance

to suppress poetic ideas which come to him—for fear that he would thereby shut off the flow of inspiration. The best of the social satires is "One Moment in Eternity." The poem focuses on the exclamations of two altar boys, who are more impressed with the luxurious Cadillac hearse outside of their church than by the grandeur of immortality that is symbolized by the funeral Mass within. The overpowering of religion is dryly signified by the chrome insignia on the tip of the car's gleaming hood, "sighting between the up/spreading wings of a silver angel taking off" (CP, 414).

The poem possesses the conciseness and urbanity that are characteristic of Gnomes & Occasions. With the exception of "The Painter Dreaming in the Scholar's House," which was composed for a public occasion, the poems show Nemerov striving for brevity in an effort to sum up. This affects both the small, exquisite nature poems and the more abstract meditations on the mind, art, and society. The unfolding explorations of earlier collections are supplanted by the compactness of retrospective vision as Nemerov screens out all but what is essential. This results in a powerful intensity and singleness of effect.

V   The Western Approaches

The Western Approaches, which appeared in 1975, came as a joyful surprise to Nemerov, who feared that he might have been drying up: "I was fully convinced that I was 'past it' through with writing and that nothing would ever happen to me again. And then suddenly in my fifty-fifth year last summer, I produced a book of poems."[18] Although the book was almost completely written in the one summer of 1974, it is a full one in comparison with Gnomes & Occasions. Nemerov commented a few years later on the unpredictable ebb and flow of the creative impetus in his case: "Writing is either easy or impossible. I can't turn a poetry crank and make it happen. I have my bad spells. But when it happens, it happens fast."[19] The mood of The Western Approaches reflects his consciousness of being "happier" and "much less introspective" than he had been in the mid-1960s, when he wrote the Journal of the Fictive Life.[20] Most of the poems are short lyrics. He had come to dislike the amplifying of some of his fellow poets, as he indicates in "Strange Metamorphosis of Poets:" "From epigram to epic is the course / For riders of the American winged horse" (CP, 451).

The title of The Western Approaches was derived from the

British name for the World War II convoy route from Iceland to Liverpool. In RAF Coastal Command Nemerov flew the half of this route closest to England in a Wellington bomber. The flights took him past the Skerries, rocky islands off the Hebrides. The Skerries are mentioned in the title poem in connection with an old Icelandic myth that depicted Hamlet as a sea god. In a letter Nemerov has explained the obscure lines about the nine maidens and the Skerries in this way: "The bit about the nine maidens grinding Hamlet's meal suggests one of those stories about how the sea turned salt after some fall from paradise in which it ground the meal for bread (and for free); in my poem I assume a second fall after which the sea ground only stone (it is reported that the rote off the Skerries can toss ninety ton boulders over (or through) the lighthouse tower."[21]

The title poem sets the mood for the collection in its preoccupation with death and entropy. The fatigue and determinism that overshadow the poem are offset, however, by the equally strong and valid perception that life is forever beginning anew:

> How a long life grows ghostly towards the close
> As any man dissolves in Everyman
> Of whom the story, as it always did, begins
> In a far country, once upon a time,
> There lived a certain man and he had three sons . . . (*CP*, 464)

The underlying-balance of the poem is upheld by the acuity of vision that enables a middle-aged man to finally understand the experience of his youth, just as Nemerov finally came to understand the meaning of the war he had fought in many years before.

The poems in *The Western Approaches* are grouped under three headings. "The Way" is the broadest of these headings and deals with the way man lives in society—as opposed to the way he ought to live. "The Ground" contains poems about nature for the most part and "The Mind" deals with the familiar themes of perception and culture. The entropic theme of the running down of the world circulates through all three sections, most conspicuously perhaps in the autumnal emphasis and in the allusions to the second law of thermodynamics.

The mood of enervation is mitigated by the underlying tone of resistance that is implicit in the opening anecdote about the dying man who refuses to listen to the revelations of the angel of death: "Among all the hosts of the dead," Nemerov notes, "he is the only one who does not know the secret of life and the meaning of the universe; whence he is held in superstitious veneration by the rest" (*CP*, 449). For Nemerov the man is an archetype of the artist, who also refuses to succumb to knowledgeable clarifications of the world by either science or religion in the face of a lingering mystery that clings to experience that has supposedly been explained.

A similar attitude of resistance surfaces caustically in poems like "He" and "Capitals," which polarize doctrinaire abstractions with the subtler, indefinite intimations that arise from experience. Thus, in attaching himself to institutionalized religion, the hero of "He" is paradoxically descibed as having "lost his faith" (*CP*, 457). As Nemerov felt himself aging and coming closer to death, he became irritable about the demands of religion, as can be seen in the biting conclusion of "Einstein & Freud & Jack": "What God wants, don't you forget it, Jack, / Is your contrite spirit, Jack, your broken heart" (*CP*, 459). The poem is a good example of Nemerov's use of the colloquial, low style.

The heavy presence of death and dying is felt in "Flower Arrangements" in which hospital patients are compared to the cut flowers that have been set next to them. The speaker ignores the conventional symbolism of the flowers in order to focus on their severed and therefore doomed state. Like the patients they are in "death already though they know it not" (*CP*, 474). The theme of death is taken up as well in the poems about autumn. "Again" is probably the most striking of the autumnal lyrics:

> And through the muted land, the nevergreen
> Needles and mull and duff of the forest floor,
> The wind go ashen, till one afternoon
> The cold snow cloud comes down the intervale
> Above the river on whose slow black flood
> The few first flakes come hurrying in to drown. (*CP*, 476)

With its impeccable imagery and finely modulated rhythm the poem recalls both the evocative settings and fluidity of the poems of the 1950s. The use of sound is particularly impressive, the muffled sounds of the "u" and short "o", which capture the apprehensiveness and stillness, skillfully set against the long "o" of the concluding lines, which signal the approach of winter and the terrifying finality of death.

Reflecting Nemerov's instinct for balance, the hand of death is usually held in check by opposing forces. In "Near the Old People's

Home," for example, the "turned-off fountain with its basin drained" is compensated for by the sparrows and the winter sun (*CP*, 478). In "Equations of a Villanelle" death, "the candle guttering to naught," is portrayed as forgiving the "breath within us for the wind without," a hopeful recognition of the beneficient continuity of being: "What if the same be true of world and thought?" (*CP*, 477). The balanced structure of the poems is nowhere better exemplified than in "A Cabinet of Seeds Displayed." The seed is one of Nemerov's emblematic symbols for the poised state between life and death that is epitomized in the moment. Trees fulfill a similar function in "The Consent." The trees are the ancient Chinese ginkgo trees whose fan-shaped leaves adorn the dust jacket and title page of *The Western Approaches*. The exoticism of the trees is balanced by their foul odor as is made clear in "Ginkgoes in Fall." The leaves of the trees, which flank the main walkway of the quadrangle at Washington University in St. Louis, enact the death of the year with a mysterious unanimity that is unrelated to temperature, wind, rain or any other visible cause: "What use," Nemerov asks, "to learn the lessons taught by time, / If a star at any time may tell us: *Now*" (*CP*, 476). The event is a humbling one in terms of human knowledge, but it does cast its own compensatory spell.

Like the seed, the tree is suspended delicately between life and death, stillness and motion, and the one and the many with the solid strength of the bole played off symbolically against the tremulous shivering of the foliage. Trees are everywhere in *The Western Approaches*, their ubiquity being a reflection of their status as one of the "shapes of our Protean nature" as Nemerov puts it in "The Thought of Trees." Since the mind itself evolved from "Protean nature," he concludes that the "trees are within us, having their quiet irrefutable / say about what we are and may become" (*CP*, 496). Similarly, in "A Common Saw" man is portrayed as bound to nature in the way King Lear was bound to the wheel of fire. Man is described as twined "round the pinkie and pinned under the thumb / Of Dame Kind dear and beautiful and dumb" (*CP*, 478).

Nature's unconscious fecundity and dominance are distinguished in *The Western Approaches* from the rigid cosmology and ossified ethics imposed by formal religion. Moreover, man is perceived as dependent upon nature, whereas, although he may in nature be a religious creature, he is viewed as having a tentative relationship to particular religious systems. His essential relationship to nature is expressed in "The Dependencies" where the speaker passively observes the nighthawks migrating south, unable to do much more about the world than attend to its beauty and violence and prepare himself for those outer and inner alterations which the seasons will inevitably bring about. Thus, seasonal fluctuations become the "private rites / And secret celebrations of the soul" as the speaker puts it in "Walking Down Westgate in the Fall" (*CP*, 474).

In spite of the thorough pessimism of poems like "Waiting Rooms" most of the poems hold to a dialectical format. Thus, the theme of erosion is characteristically offset by a depiction of life's resilience. This can be seen in the use of the motif of the second law of thermodynamics, which focuses on the irreversible loss of heat through the expenditure of energy—the running down of the world; "We're going to our doom in supreme comfort, compared to any other world you could name."[22] The second law is pictured as at least temporarily halted, however, in poems like "Drawing Lessons" where water, as opposed to land, has the "wondrous property / And power of assembling itself again / When shattered" so that the second law "seems to reverse itself, (*CP*, 498). The land with its "decay, and dust that blows away" becomes a symbol of the empirical world. The sea, on the other hand, a symbol of the imagination and of the recesses of being that lie beyond knowledge, is portrayed as a "little more mysterious than that." The poem thus affirms the spirit and its freedom from the attrition implicit in the second law of thermodynamics.

Nemerov sees the entropic process of the second law as balanced to a limited extent by the conclusions of Darwin.[23] Darwin's scenario of the spiraling evolution of being means that if the universe is running down in most fundamental respects it is also simultaneously throwing up higher forms of life. The pull of the second law is dominant, however, as can be seen in "Route Two" with its absurd billboard message—"Save While You Spend"—which Nemerov passed while driving along a secondary highway: "As if one saw / A way to beat the Second Law / By pouring money down the drain / As long as it was one's own drain" (*CP*, 456). "Playing Skittles" and "Gyroscope" describe a delicate navigational instrument, which becomes another Nemerovian symbol of stillness in motion. The gyroscope's "unshivering integrity" makes it appear to be in an apparent state of perpetual motion, but it eventually wobbles and "drops dead into its own skeleton"(*CP*, 501).

An analogous decline is visualized in "First Snow" with the world eventually becoming enshrouded in a final snow that seals the "sleepy cities up, / Filling their deep and canyoned avenues / Forever" (*CP*, 480). Here, though, the speaker resiliently shrugs off the feeling of portent as an example of nineteenth-century hysteria and focuses instead on the present moment with its softly falling snow that "hisses through the whitening grass, / And rattles among the few remaining leaves." In "Two Pair" the first and second laws of thermodynamics are interlaced with the Mosaic first and Christian second laws of religion in ironic symmetry. Playing on the theme of conservation that is implicit in the first law of thermodynamics, Nemerov writes: "The first pair tells us we may be redeemed, / But in a world, the other says, that's doomed" (*CP*, 457). The poem implies that the hopeful vision of the Jews, the old law, was somehow lost amidst the mortifications of its Christian sequel.

A number of the poems employ elaborate scientific conceits. The laws of relativity are applied with great metaphorical freedom in "Fugue," which attempts to illuminate the human perception of time. Because of the close relationship between music and mathematics the title of the poem has the effect of reconciling discrete kinds of perception and experience. The poems are studded with occasional metaphors that reflect a scientific perspective. In "Figures of Thought," for example, the mind's capacity to discover analogies is pictured as the laying of a "logarithmic spiral on / Sea-shell and leaf alike, and see it fit" (*CP*, 472).

In general Nemerov's view of science is fairly tough minded in spite of his reliance on it in the later poems. In "Seeing Things" the narrator has a view of a marsh on a summer evening that strikes him as the closest he has ever come to "seeing things / The way the physicists say things really are" (*CP*, 479). What he sees is a ring of smoke around a tree that gives it the appearance of being on fire but which when looked at through binoculars turns out to be a cloud of gnats:

> Their millions doing such a steady dance
> As by the motion of the many made the one
> Shape constant and kept it so in both the forms
> I'd thought to see, the fire and the tree.
> Strike through the mask? you find another mask,
> Mirroring mirrors by analogy
> Make visible. I watched till the greater smoke
> Of night engulfed the other, standing out

> On the marsh amid a hundred hidden streams
> Meandering down from Concord to the sea. (*CP*, 479 - 80)

The binoculars appear to dramatize the corrective vision of science. In the conclusion, however, science is seen as just another "mask." Furthermore, the enlarged perspective of the final lines places both the ordinary vision of the eye and the mechanical vision of the binoculars against a background whose cosmic mysteriousness outweighs the differences between the eye and the telescope.

In "Einstein & Freud & Jack" science is described as beginning and ending "in myth" (*CP*, 459). Nemerov's irreverence toward science reaches its nadir in "Cosmic Comics": "Where Moses saw the seat of God / Science has seen what's just as odd, / The asshole of the universe" (*CP*, 451). If formal religion fails because of its rigidity, science fails in the gross application of its methods to reality. Nevertheless, Nemerov appreciates the freshness of the perspectives provided by science. In "The Weather of the World," for example, satellite cameras literally capture the face of the planet giving it an unexpected affective dimension:

> Containing contradictions, tempers, moods,
> Able to be serene, gloomy or mad,
> Liable to huge explosions, brooding in
> Depressions over several thousand miles
> In length and trailing tears in floods of sorrow
> That drown the counties and the towns. (*CP*, 483)

Reflecting a similar originality in perspective, in "The Backward Look" satellite man looks back longingly to earth, a "small blue agate in the big black bag" and hopes for a safe return from the precariousness of space in the "hand / Of mathematics" (*CP*, 470).

When liberated from scientism, science becomes simply another pathway for the mind, whose powers are celebrated in the final section of *The Western Approaches*. In "There" and "The Spy" the immense mysteries of space and the earth are compared paradoxically with the comparatively minuscule arena of the skull:

> Behind the brow, a scant deep inch away,
> The little nutshell mystery meditates
> The spiral fire of the soul;
> Through eyes as innocent and wide as day
> It spies upon the true appearances of
> Our sensible old world. (*CP*, 502 - 03)

By expanding the size of the eye to be as "wide as day" in the final lines, Nemerov manages metaphorically to dramatize the awesome power of the "nutshell" eye and cerebrum.

Nemerov not only abandons his pessimism about the mind's limitations in *The Western Approaches,* but he suggests in poems like "TV," which deals playfully with idealistic metaphysics, that all life depends on someone's looking at it, just as the world on television implies a cameraman. Similarly, the fictional universe in "Reflexion of a Novelist" depends upon a sustaining ultimate consciousness. Such an ultimate consciousness could never be understood by the characters in a novel, nor by living men, for that matter, because of the very nature of creation—their creator "hovering there / A dimension past the space in which they speak" (*CP*, 483). The mind's creativity is honored in a number of poems, notably in "The Makers," "Plane," "Conversing with Paradise," "The Four Ages," and ""Playing the Inventions." In "Playing the Inventions" Nemerov marvels at the sublime fugues of Bach. The music reflects the adventurousness of a mind that "cannot know / Except by modeling what it would know" (*CP*, 489). Having thus struck out into new territory, the mind of Bach curves back upon its new theme and upon itself in a pattern in which the melody's "sides and the roof and floor are mirrors / With some device that will reflect in time / As mirrors do in space."

The mirror motif lacks the pessimism that characterized Nemerov's earlier epistemological excursions. One reason for this is that the mind's reflexive curving upon itself, which underlies art, is perceived as analogous to the shape of external reality. In "The Metaphysical Automobile" the shortest way between two points on the earth, the speaker explains, happens to be a curve:

> And so do song
> And story, winding crank and widdershins,
> Still get there first, and poetry remains
> Eccentric and odd and riddling and right,
> Eternal return of the excluded middle. (*CP*, 453)

In these late poems Nemerov simply recognizes that it is mind that had chiefly captured his interest all along and that the vast brow of the external world pales in comparison with the mind that illuminates it. Therefore, the moments of reflexiveness that had interrupted earlier poetic meditations here become the principal subject. In a sense Nemerov's life finally becomes his art, an art which holds out the prospect of paradisal vision and a refuge from the sterile neutralities of the empirical world. Even the poems about society seem to be as much about the mind of the narrator as about external behavior, as is evident in the anthropological ruminations of "Watching Football on TV" and the garrulous pronouncements of "The Metaphysical Automobile."

In its preoccupation with various kinds of laws, *The Western Approaches* brings Nemerov's poetry full circle. Like *The Image and the Law* and indeed like most of the subsequent collections *The Western Approaches* revolves around the central philosophical question of the one and the many. The function of the law is somehow to reconcile the concrete particulars of experience with the generalizing and abstracting habits of the mind without losing sight of the sensuous individuality of things. By the time Nemerov gets to *The Western Approaches*, the phenomenal world has become as much a part of an enveloping cosmic dream as the laws drawn from it. While taking care to preserve the concreteness and individuality of phenomena, Nemerov is no longer haunted by the question of their epistemological validity.

Stylistically as well there are resemblances between *The Western Approaches* and *The Image and the Law*. The use of formal metaphors and conceits is a noticeable link between the two volumes. Poems like "Late Summer" and "A Cabinet of Seeds Displayed" in *The Western Approaches* are obvious examples. The acorns in "Late Summer" are portrayed as wearing "neat berets," while the horse chestnuts are "shiny as shoes inside their spiny husks, / Prickly planets among the sweetgum's starry leaves" (*CP*, 473). In "A Cabinet of Seeds Displayed" the seeds are fancifully depicted as the "original monies of the earth, / In which invested, as the spark in fire, / They will produce a green wealth toppling tall" (*CP*, 473). Similarly, in "An Ending" the mind is pictured as subdued by the later summer rain going forth a "penitent in a shroud of grey / To walk the sidewalks that reflect the sky" (*CP*, 506). The stylistic hyperbole mirrors Nemerov's confident attitude toward the play of the mind. Freed from the need to conceal itself in the shapes of the external world, the imagination in the later poems rejoices in a frank display of its powers.

CHAPTER 5

A *Final Approach*

O NE reason for the neglect of Nemerov's writings in the 1950s and 1960s is that he avoided involving himself in social and political issues in a period when this sort of commitment was fashionable. His restraint was partly philosophical. He objected to the arrogance of poets promulgating their social views in the name of art. In addition, though, he felt instinctively that he had confronted the ultimate social ordeal in World War II. His participation in the war in fact prevented him from taking subsequent events seriously, as he acknowledged in a letter he wrote to Kay Boyle in 1967:

Maybe my trouble with history was that at first I didn't believe in it; from my boyhood in the Depression history was separated by the deep and absolute trench of the First War; then when the Second War brought it to my compulsory notice, and when we got through that viciously necessary orgy, I guess I accepted—and was not alone in doing so—a rather simplified story of how with the passing of Hitler evil itself had gone out of the world; a story so incredible it need only be summarized to be smiled at.[1]

A further reason for the belated recognition of Nemerov's worth can be found in his quiet and resolute resistance to sentimentality and in his forthright pursuit of complex forms, both of which have discouraged different but equally large groups of readers. Furthermore, his subject matter has appeared to many to be overly erudite and esoteric. His general reputation up until the 1960s, then, was of a cloistered academic who spent a lot of his time in trying to perfect obsolete forms of prose and verse. While there is some truth in this assessment, it is gradually becoming clear that Nemerov has been extracting ore whose value has only recently been realized. Beneath the social turbulence of the 1950s and 1960s lies an intellectual and moral break with the past that he has convincingly described as

fundamentally epistemological. Thrown back upon his own
resources by a culture that is no longer able to guide him, contemporary man is depicted in Nemerov as sustaining what had been
known as civilization by developing individual consciousness. Both
the pathos and excitement of Nemerov's writings come from his un-
flinching view of the isolated self trying to piece together the world
on its own.

Unlike the narrator of Eliot's *Waste Land*, who gathers together
the available rubble of Western culture in an attempt to reach a
satisfactory synthesis, Nemerov's poetic narrators have an even
greater skepticism about the past than about the present. As a consequence they are driven to invent and thereby to discover the
nature of the world they inhabit. In the early volumes the process
seems futile and unsubstantial even if imaginative. Later, imperceptibly, the poems begin to imply with a relaxed acceptance that the
world seen by the eye and the mind is the only world worth knowing. For some readers the reflexive poetry will seem a remote subject that Nemerov has seen fit to focus on in the absence of other experience. Indeed, he has sometimes talked about writing in this
way.[2] In addition to the pleasure he derives from writing, however,
he upholds the Muse as the mapmaker of the mind, the mind in
turn being a map of the world—possibly an illusory world—but the
only world we are ever likely to know.

Introspection is not a mood in Nemerov's work. It is the very atmosphere of his world, which becomes finally a corridor of
mirrors—like the great hall at Versailles—in which the mind is seen
gliding through the void. Searching for friendship, the mind finds
only itself. Trying on the shapes of the external world in an unending masquerade, the mind finds fascination and satisfaction, if
not companionship, in creatures that are, metaphysically, at least,
smaller than itself. The most abiding of these creatures are found in
the natural world. Few of the poems concern Nemerov's
relationship with people and even the novels and short stories portray people from a distance. Nemerov has discussed his reticence
about drawing on personal relationships in the *Journal of the Fictive Life*. When he does write about personal relationships, as in the
poem about his sister's suicide in *Gnomes & Occasions*, his approach is restrained and indirect—even if ultimately moving.

Nemerov's writings about man in society frequently suggest a
mind that is coolly disengaged. Although this has not prevented
him, as has been pointed out, from writing some distinguished

novels and poems, it does perhaps call for some final comment. Nemerov's compassion for his fellow man is tempered by a deep-seated skepticism. This can be seen in the letter to Kay Boyle previously quoted in which he set forth his reaction to the prolonged American war in Vietnam: "The damn war, and all the rest of it, has me paralyzed. I read the papers with terrible fascination in which nevertheless there is an element of mockery. More and more I seem to see something about tragedy which always puzzled me and made me mistrust this supposed highest art form—that the tragic flaw, so long dignified in translations of the Poetics as 'pride' or, more mildly, 'error,' is in its essence something more like simple Stupidity" (August 12, 1967).

Nemerov's supposed narrowness is simply a reflection of his cultivated pursuit of what interests and preoccupies him as a poet and novelist. He is a contemplative writer whose primary interest is in the process of contemplation itself. No modern writer has more eloquently traced the subtle emanations of consciousness and its shadowy journeying through the fine membrane of language out into the strangeness of the external world. In this connection he told an interviewer in 1966 that possibly the "only significance that anyone was ever able to rely on, in thought at any rate, was the love of the world, terrifying as it is, that connected him to it by means of the word."[3] In retrospect the novels, stories, and poems coalesce in the light of this observation. His interest has continually been in the excitement caused when the pliable but domineering mind comes up against the hard surface of the external world. With breadth of vision he has shown the results of this collision to be simultaneously pathetic and absurd. The pathos and absurdity are symbolic of a whole range of ambivalences that allow one to see Nemerov as a religious poet with no religion, a philosophical poet with no philosophy, and a satirist filled with compassion.

Nemerov's strength lies in the persuasiveness with which he articulates these ambivalences and in the clarity with which he brings the complex refractions of consciousness within vivid reach of the senses. Paradoxically, it is often his most cerebral poems that engage the senses most provocatively, as in "The Town Dump" and "Brainstorm." It is as if in his lifelong effort to unite inner and outer worlds he stretches himself on such occasions to sustain the fine balance between the sensible and the immaterial. In both poetry and prose he has shown an absorbing interest in the experimenting mind. Challenged by the monotony of their society and by the obdurate silence of the physical world, his fictional characters and poetic narrators react to their plight with originality and panache. Nemerov gives them depth, moreover, in revealing the disaffection and hunger that linger after their most brilliant intellectual excursions. In this respect as in others, Nemerov has, without especially trying to do so, trenchantly captured the spirit of his time.

Notes and References

Chapter One

1. Note attached to the broadside poem "Small Moment," published by Poems in Folio (San Francisco, 1957).
2. "An Interview with Howard Nemerov," *Island*, 4, (November 1966), 2.
3. *Journal of the Fictive Life* (New Brunswick, N.J., 1963), p. 17.
4. Donald Crinklaw, "Vibrations of a Literary Misanthrope," *St. Louisan*, September 1975, p. 69.
5. *Journal of the Fictive Life*, p. 123.
6. Ibid., p. 108.
7. Ibid., p. 62.
8. Ibid., p. 84.
9. "An Interview with Howard Nemerov," *Island*, 4:8.
10. "An Occident Symposium," *Occident*, 3 (Summer 1969), 104.
11. "Speculation Turning to Itself," *Prose*, 3 (Fall 1971), 99.
12. "Poetry and the National Conscience," *Reflexions on Poetry & Poetics* (hereafter abbreviated *Reflexions*; New Brunswick, N.J., 1972), pp. 149 - 50.
13. "The Muse's Interest," *Poetry & Fiction* (New Brunswick, N.J., 1963), p. 47.
14. "Two Ways of the Imagination: Blake & Wordsworth," *Reflexions*, p. 106.
15. "Two Gentlemen of Verona: A Commentary," *Poetry & Fiction*, p. 29.
16. *Reflexions*, p. 221.
17. "Speculation Turning," 93.
18. Quoted in Robert D. Harvey, "A Prophet Armed: An Introduction to the Poetry of Howard Nemerov," *Poets in Progress*, ed. H. B. Hungerford (Chicago, 1967), p. 125.
19. *Journal of the Fictive Life*, p. 21.
20. *Christian Century*, 85 (November 27, 1968), 1502.
21. "The Sweeper of Ways," *Reflexions*, p. 160.
22. "The Agon of Will as Idea," *Furioso*, 2 (Spring 1947), 30 - 31.
23. *Reflexions*, pp. 165 - 66.
24. *Poetry & Fiction*, p. 11.
25. *Reflexions*, p. 232.
26. "The Swaying Form," *Poetry & Fiction*, p. 12.

27. "On Poetry and Painting with a Thought of Music," *Prose*, 3 (Fall 1971), 101.

28. "An Interview with Howard Nemerov," *Island*, 4:5.

29. *Reflexions*, p. 209.

30. Ibid., p. 86.

31. *Journal of the Fictive Life*, p. 68.

32. "Poetry & Meaning," *Salmagundi*, 22 - 23 (1973), 44.

33. *Reflexions*, p. 218.

34. *Poetry & Fiction*, p. 102.

35. *Reflexions*, p. 16.

36. *Poetry & Fiction*, p. 11.

37. *The Carleton Miscellany*, I (Winter 1960), 36. Reprinted in *The Collected Poems of Howard Nemerov* (Chicago and London, 1977), p. 492.

38. *Reflexions*, p. 145.

39. *Poetry & Fiction*, p. 165.

40. *Reflexions*, p. 169.

41. Ibid., p. 72.

42. Ibid., p. 165.

43. Ibid., p. 30.

44. Note attached to the broadside poem "Small Moment," published by Poems in Folio (San Francisco, 1957).

45. Quoted in Harvey, "A Prophet Armed," p. 125.

46. "Thirteen Ways of Looking at a Skylark," *Poetry*, 126 (August 1975), 297.

47. *Reflexions*, p. 44.

48. "Poetry & Meaning," p. 43.

Chapter Two

1. *A Commodity of Dreams & Other Stories* (New York, 1959). Page references appear in the text.

2. *Journal of the Fictive Life*, p. 31.

3. *Stories, Fables & Other Diversions* (Boston, 1971). Page references appear in the text.

4. *Journal of the Fictive Life*, p. 61.

5. *The Melodramatists* (New York, 1949). Page references appear in the text.

6. *Poetry & Fiction*, p. 249.

7. *The Next Room of the Dream* (Chicago, 1962). Reprinted in *The Collected Poems of Howard Nemerov* (Chicago and London, 1977), p. 272.

8. Crinklaw, p. 66.

9. "The Nature of Novels," *Partisan Review*, 24 (Fall 1957), 605.

10. *Journal of the Fictive Life*, p. 61.

11. *Federigo, or the Power of Love* (Boston and Toronto, 1954). Page references appear in the text.

12. *Journal of the Fictive Life*, p. 61.

13. Ibid., p. 15. The Warner Brothers film was called *Tall Story* and featured Anthony Perkins, with Jane Fonda in her starring debut. A comparison of the novel and the film is made in Robert L. White's "The Trying-out of 'The Homecoming Game,' " *Colorado Quarterly*, 10 (Spring 1959), 84 - 96.

14. *The Homecoming Game* (New York, 1957). Page references appear in the text.

15. See Nemerov's unsigned essay "Football" in *Furioso*, 6 (Spring 1951), 66 - 68.

16. Nemerov introduced Felix Ledger in the sketch "From a Novel as Yet Untitled," *Furioso*, 6 (Summer 1951), 11 - 22.

17. *Journal of the Fictive Life* (New Brunswick, N.J., 1965). Page references in the following pages of this chapter appear in the text.

18. Letter to Margot Johnson, November 16, 1963.

19. Crinklaw, 66.

Chapter Three

1. *Journal of the Fictive Life*, pp. 21, 20.

2. Crinklaw, p. 54.

3. Robert Boyers, "An Interview with Howard Nemerov," *Salmagundi*, 31 - 32 (Fall 1975 and Winter 1976), 116.

4. Ibid., p. 109.

5. *Island*, 4:2 - 3.

6. *The Collected Poems of Howard Nemerov* (Chicago and London, 1977). Page references throughout the text will be to this collection and are incorporated into the text, labeled "CP."

7. *Island*, 4:4.

8. Crinklaw, p. 54.

9. "Observations of an Alien," *New Republic*, June 23, 1958, p. 27.

10. Boyers, p. 112.

11. Nemerov, in composing "Zalmoxis," drew upon Rhys Carpenter, *Folk Tale, Fiction, Saga in Homeric Epics* (Berkeley and Los Angeles, 1946); see especially pp. 112 - 14.

12. *Journal of the Fictive Life*, p. 108.

13. "Comments on Eighteen Poems by Howard Nemerov," *Sewanee Review*, 60 (Winter 1952), 117 - 31.

14. *Journal of the Fictive Life*, p. 90.

15. Ibid., p. 121.

16. *Island*, 4:2.

17. Quoted in Linda Jean Knight, "A Study of Howard Nemerov's Lan-

guage as It Reflects the Theme of Time in His Poetry" (unpublished Master's thesis, University of Vermont, 1967), p. x.

18. Boyers, pp. 117 - 18.

Chapter Four

1. *Poet's Choice*, ed. Paul Engle and Joseph Lang (New York, 1962), p. 186.

2. Ibid.

3. *Reflexions*, p. 87.

4. Loosely translated, the epigraph reads, "While in good health, I was overcome by madness, and while filled with life, I was dying."

5. *Reflexions*, p. 172.

6. Letter to the author, July 29, 1978.

7. *Journal of the Fictive Life*, p. 152.

8. Ibid., p. 170.

9. Author's conversation with Nemerov, May 1977.

10. *Reflexions*, pp. 154 - 55.

11. Nemerov comments on this phenomenon in "Attentiveness & Obedience," *Reflexions*, p. 171.

12. "Showdown at City of Poetry," "Book Week," *Chicago Sun-Times*, December 3, 1967, p. 5.

13. Introduction to Owen Barfield's *Poetic Diction* (New York, 1964), p. 3.

14. *Reflexions*, p. 162.

15. Ibid., p. 40.

16. Paul Wagman, "Profound Master of 'Plain' Poetry," *St. Louis Post-Dispatch*, November 11, 1973, Sec. H, p. 3.

17. Quoted in Julia Bartholomay, *The Shield of Perseus: The Vision and Imagination of Howard Nemerov* (Gainesville, Fla., 1972), p. 154.

18. Crinklaw, p. 52.

19. *W. U. Record* (Washington University, St. Louis), May 19, 1977, p. 2.

20. Crinklaw, pp. 66 - 68.

21. Letter to the author, July 29, 1978. Nemerov came upon the reference to Hamlet as a sea god in Israel Gollancz's *The Sources of Hamlet*.

22. Crinklaw, p. 69.

23. Author's conversation with Nemerov, May, 1977.

Chapter Five

1. Unpublished letter to Kay Boyle, Aug. 12, 1967.

2. *Island*, 4:2 - 3.

3. Ibid., 4:3.

Selected Bibliography

PRIMARY SOURCES

1. Collected Works

The Collected Poems of Howard Nemerov. Chicago and London: University of Chicago Press, 1977. (Throughout the text page references to this volume are identified by the abbreviation *CP*.)

2. Poems

The Blue Swallows. Chicago and London: University of Chicago Press, 1967.
Gnomes & Occasions. Chicago and London: University of Chicago Press, 1973.
Guide to the Ruins. New York: Random House, 1950.
The Image and the Law. New York: Henry Holt, 1947.
Mirrors & Windows. Chicago: University of Chicago Press, 1958.
New & Selected Poems. Chicago and London: University of Chicago Press, 1960.
The Next Room of the Dream. Chicago; University of Chicago Press, 1962.
The Salt Garden. Boston and Toronto: Little, Brown, 1953.
The Western Approaches. Chicago and London: University of Chicago Press, 1975.

3. Novels

Federigo, or The Power of Love. Boston: Little, Brown, 1954.
The Homecoming Game. New York: Simon and Schuster, 1957.
The Melodramatists. New York: Random House, 1949.

4. Short Stories

A Commodity of Dreams & Other Stories. New York: Simon and Schuster, 1959.
Stories, Fables & Other Diversions. Boston: Godine, 1971.

5. Essays

Poetry & Fiction: Essays. New Brunswick, N.J.: Rutgers University Press, 1963.
Reflexions on Poetry & Poetics. New Brunswick, N.J.: Rutgers University Press, 1972.

6. Autobiography

Journal of the Fictive Life. New Brunswick, N.J.: Rutgers University Press, 1965.

7. Articles

"The Agon of Will as Idea," *Furioso*, 2 (Spring 1947), 29 - 42.

"Composition and Fate in the Short Novel," *Perspectives in Contemporary Criticism*, ed. Sheldon Grebstein. New York: Harper and Row, 1968, pp. 120 - 32.

"The Measure of Poetry," *Carleton Miscellany*, 1 (Winter 1960), 32-36.

"On Going Down in History," *Christian Century*, 135 (November 27, 1968), 1500 - 1503.

"On Poetry and Painting, with a Thought of Music," *Prose*, 3 (Fall 1971), 101 - 108.

"On the Resemblances between Science and Religion," *The Rarer Action*, ed. Alan Cheuse and Richard Koffler. New Brunswick, N.J.: Rutgers University Press, 1970, pp. 333 - 39.

"Poetry and History," *Virginia Quarterly Review*, 51 (1975), 309 - 28.

"Poetry and Meaning," *Salmagundi*, 22 - 23 (1973), 42 - 56.

"Speculation Turning to Itself," *Prose*, 3 (Fall 1971), 89 - 99.

SECONDARY SOURCES

1. Books, Pamphlets, and Dissertations

BARTHOLOMAY, JULIE A. *The Shield of Perseus: The Vision and Imagination of Howard Nemerov.* Gainesville, Florida: The University of Florida Press, 1972. The book concentrates on Nemerov's poetic imagery. Bartholomay was the first to write about the elaborate structure of "Runes."

DUNCAN, BOWIE. *The Critical Reception of Howard Nemerov: A Selection of Essays and a Bibliography.* Metuchen, New Jersey: The Scarecrow Press, 1971. An invaluable book. Makes accessible a number of important essays and reviews, and contains a concise and helpful introduction to Nemerov's work by Reed Whittemore. Essays include: Julia Randall, "Genius of the Shore: The Poetry of Howard Nemerov," pp. 14 - 28; Peter Meinke, "Twenty Years of Accomplishment," pp. 29 - 39; Robert Harvey, "A Prophet Armed: An Introduction to the Poetry of Howard Nemerov," pp. 40 - 55; and Donna Gerstenberger, "An Interview with Howard Nemerov," pp. 56 - 61. Except for the essay by Harvey, which is available in book form, copies of the other essays are not easy to obtain. This applies in the main as well to the many reviews of Nemerov's work reprinted by Duncan.

GILLUM, JOHN MICHAEL. "Mind, World, and Word in the Poetry of Howard Nemerov." Ph.D. dissertation, University of Wisconsin, Madison, 1974. A perceptive analysis of Nemerov's interest in epistemological questions.

MEINKE, PETER. *Howard Nemerov*. UMPAW 70. Minneapolis: University of Minnesota Press, 1968. A reliable, concise overview of both poetry and fiction up to 1968.

MILLS, WILLIAM. *The Stillness in Moving Things: The World of Howard Nemerov*. Memphis: Memphis State University Press, 1975. Relates Nemerov's poetry to recent philosophical movements.

2. Articles

BURKE, KENNETH. "Comments on Eighteen Poems by Howard Nemerov." *Sewanee Review*, 60 (Winter 1952), 117 - 31. An imaginative reading of "The Scales of the Eyes."

DICKEY, JAMES. "Howard Nemerov," in *Babel to Byzantium: Poets and Poetry Now*. New York: Farrar, Straus and Giroux, 1960, pp. 35 - 41. Reprint of an earlier review of *The Salt Garden*. Useful as an early view of Nemerov's poetry.

HARVEY, ROBERT D. "A Prophet Armed: An Introduction to the Poetry of Howard Nemerov," in *Poets in Progress*. Ed. E. B. Hungerford. Chicago: Northwestern University Press, 1967, pp. 116 - 33. Examines the motifs of war, the city, and nature.

KIEHL, JAMES M. "The Poems of Howard Nemerov: Where Loveliness Adorns Intelligible Things." *Salmagundi*, 22 - 23 (1973), 234 - 57. A general appreciation of Nemerov's poetry.

MEINKE, PETER. "Twenty Years of Accomplishment." *Florida Quarterly*, 1 (October 1968), 81 - 90. Good analysis of Nemerov's development from the early poems to *The Blue Swallows*.

RANDALL, JULIA. "Genius of the Shore: The Poetry of Howard Nemerov." *Hollins Critic*, 6 (1969), 1 - 12. Incisive study of Nemerov's imagery.

SMITH, RAYMOND. "Nemerov and Nature: The Stillness in Moving Things." *Southern Review*, 10 (1974), 153 - 69. Sensitive analysis of Nemerov's reflexive approach to poetry.

WHITE, ROBERT L. "The Trying-out of 'The Homecoming Game,'" *Colorado Quarterly*, 10 (1959), 84 - 96. Interesting comparison of the novel and film.

WHITTEMORE, REED. "Observations of an Alien." *New Republic*, June 23, 1958, pp. 27 - 28. Valuable commentary by Nemerov's friend and former colleague.

3. Interviews

BOYERS, ROBERT. "An Interview with Howard Nemerov." *Salmagundi*, 31 - 32 (Fall 1975 - Winter 1976), 109 - 19. Subtle, esoteric discussion of poetic form.

CARGAS, HARRY J. "An Interview with Howard Nemerov." *Webster Review*, 1 (1974), 34 - 39. Nemerov discusses literary influences on his work.

CRINKLAW, DONALD. "Vibrations of a Literary Misanthrope." *St. Louisan*,

September, 1975, pp. 52 - 55, 66 - 69. Nemerov interviewed at Washington University in St. Louis. Wide range of topics—writing and teaching, trends in recent American poetry, poetry and religion. A valuable source though difficult to obtain.

GERSTENBERGER, DONNA. "An Interview with Howard Nemerov." *Trace*, 35 (January-February 1960), 22 - 25. Nemerov's views on poetry and academia.

"An Interview with Howard Nemerov." *Island*, November 1966, pp. 2 - 8. Some eloquent comments on the nature of poetry. Important source but difficult to obtain.

"An Occident Symposium." *Occident*, 3 (Summer 1969), 101 - 13. On poetry and the imagination.

Index

155